The Forty Hadith of al-Imam an-Nawawi

Completed by

Umm Muhammad

TABLE OF CONTENTS

Preface i
Al-Imām an-Nawawi ii
"And Whatever the Messenger Has Given You – Take" iv

The Forty Ḥadīth

No.	Subject	Page no.
1	Importance of intention	1
2	Definition of Islām, īmān and iḥsān	4
3	Pillars of Islam	8
4	Man's development and final deeds	10
5	Prohibition of innovation in religion	13
6	Avoidance of doubtful matters	15
7	Religion is sincerity	17
8	Protection of Muslims	19
9	Obedience to the Prophet (ﷺ)	21
10	Limiting oneself to what is lawful	23
11	Adherence to what is certain	25
12	Refining the soul	26
13	Consideration for others	28
14	Legal execution	29
15	Good character	32
16	Anger	34
17	Proficiency in slaughter	36
18	Avoiding sins	37
19	One's relationship with Allah	39
20	Shame and shyness	42
21	Upright conduct	43
22	Religious obligations lead to Paradise	44
23	Good deeds	45
24	Some attributes of Allah	47
25	Rewards	51
26	Charities	53

27	Righteousness and wrongdoing	54
28	Instruction	56
29	Ways to Paradise	58
30	Rights of Allah (*subḥānahu wa ta'ālā*)	61
31	Indifference to worldly things	63
32	Prohibition of all harm	66
33	Evidence	68
34	Prohibiting wrong	70
35	Social behavior	73
36	Relieving a Muslim brings aid from Allah	77
37	Allah's generosity	81
38	Allah's anger and approval	85
39	Errors overlooked by Allah	88
40	Reducing worldly aspirations	91
41	Faith is love of obedience	94
42	Allah's capacity for forgiveness	96

PREFACE

All praise is due to Allah (*subḥānahu wa ta'ālā*), of whom we ask blessings and peace upon His final prophet, Muḥammad .

The collection of *Forty* Ḥadīth compiled by al-Imām Yaḥya bin Sharaf an-Nawawi (which actually contains 42 ḥadīths) has been widely studied in traditional Arabic circles of learning and continues to be one of the basic subjects taught in Islamic courses throughout the world today. This is primarily due to:

1) the soundness of the collection as a whole – most of its narrations having been taken from the two "*Ṣaḥeeḥs*" of al-Bukhāri and Muslim,
2) the conciseness and comprehensiveness of the prophetic statements contained therein, and
3) the fact that from them are derived many of the basic principles of *`aqeedah* and *sharī`ah.*

A translation into English of *An-Nawawi's Forty Ḥadīth* by Ezzeddin Ibrahim and Denys Johnson-Davies was first published in 1976 and has since then enjoyed numerous reprints. Although a faithful translation, it is limited to the text of each ḥadīth. Al-Imām an-Nawawi had himself included some explanatory annotation, and numerous scholars subsequently contributed further explanation and commentary on *An-Nawawi's Forty* in Arabic. Most of this material, however, has remained inaccessible to those without knowledge of the language.

In an attempt to fill this gap and assist more people toward an understanding of these ḥadīths and the religion in general, a few of the better known and accepted explanations by early scholars have been compiled and abridged for the benefit of English readers. The original translation of the text (*matn*) of the ḥadīth by Ibrahim and Johnson-Davies has been slightly altered in places for the purpose of clarification or accuracy. Explanatory commentary is based upon that of al-Imām an-Nawawi himself, as well as the concise *Sharḥ* of Ibn Daqeeq al-'Eed (d. 702 H.) and the more detailed *Jāmi' ul-'Ulūm wal-Ḥikam* by al-Imām Ibn Rajab (d. 795 H.).

This modest work is submitted for the acceptance of Allah (*subḥānahu wa ta'ālā*) and with hope that it will prove useful to His servants.

AL-IMĀM AN-NAWAWI

Abū Zakariyya Yaḥyā Sharaf an-Nawawi was born in the town of an-Nawā, south of Damascus, in the year of Hijrah 631, corresponding to 1233 of the Gregorian calendar. He was encouraged from childhood by his father toward religious scholarship, and so strong was his love for Qur'ānic studies that he refused to be distracted by other boys urging him to play. At the age of nineteen his father took him to Damascus, which was then a prominent seat of learning and accommodated the best scholars of his time.

An-Nawawi recalls that for the first two years of study under his shaykh, al-Kamāl al-Maghrabi, he hardly ate or slept while devoting himself to the memorization and understanding of volumes of *fiqh,* and later, under other distinguished scholars, those of ḥadīth, fundamentals of religion, Arabic language and other related specialties. He never tired of reading and writing, allowing himself to rest only when sleep overcame him during a limited portion of the night and then quickly awakening to continue his work. During this six year period he was examined daily in eleven lessons pertaining to various subjects.

Al-Imām an-Nawawi was blessed with an exceptional memory coupled with such insight and understanding that enabled him to put together and assess all that he had read at different times from various sources. Additionally, he embodied the Islamic traits of modesty, patience and courage in support of the truth. He practiced counsel and advice in a manner that people found acceptable and positive.

Although he studied in depth the *fiqh* of other *madh·habs* and their sources, an-Nawawi considered himself to be of the Shāfi'i school and was in fact among the prominent scholars of that *madh·hab.* This did not prevent him, however, from advocating adherence to a sound ḥadīth even though it might be contrary to the knowledge of the Shāfi'i scholars or even to al-Imām ash-Shāfi'i himself. This was clearly stated in his *Fatāwā.* He was also among the strongest opponents of *bid`ah* (innovations in religion) and wrote: "Know that the correct choice is that which was practiced by the *salaf...* and do not be deceived by the great numbers who differ from it."[1]

The Imām authored a great number of books in various disciplines, including *fiqh,* ḥadīth and its sciences, Arabic definition, and biography, all of which are outstanding in expression and precision. His easy, yet eloquent style, was something uncommon to his age and was appreciated by his successors. Among the best known of his works in the field of *fiqh* are:

Rawḏḥat at-Ṭālibeen (12 volumes)

Al-Minhāj

Al-Majmū` (9 volumes but incomplete due to his death)

Fatāwā (collected by his student, 'Ala'uddeen al-'Aṭṭār)

---

1 *Al-Adhkār,* p. 136.

Those in the field of ḥadīth are:

Sharḥ Saḥeeḥ Muslim, an explanation of and commentary on Muslim's collection

Riyā<u>dh</u> aṣ-Ṣāliḥeen, a collection of *aḥādeeth* pertaining to faith, one's relationship with Allah and righteous conduct

Al-Adhkār, a collection of supplications from the Qur'ān and sunnah

Al-Arba'ūn, the "Forty Ḥadīth"

An-Nawawi remained for 28 years in Damascus, studying and teaching. In the year 676 H. he returned all the books he had borrowed and visited his colleagues from among the shaykhs and the graves of those of them who had passed on. He then returned to his home in an-Nawā, where shortly thereafter he became ill and died at the age of forty-five. The city of Damascus was shaken by the news of his death, and Muslims everywhere mourned the loss of a unique scholar – may Allah have mercy upon him.

بسم الله الرحمن الرحيم

"AND WHATEVER THE MESSENGER HAS GIVEN YOU – TAKE"

(Sūrah al-Ḥashr, 59:7)

(An introduction by al-Imām an-Nawawi)

Praise is [due] to Allah, Lord of the worlds, Sustainer of the heavens and the earths, director of created beings, sender of messengers (may Allah's blessings and peace be upon them all) to responsible beings[2] in order to guide them and clarify the ways of religion by means of decisive evidences and clear proofs. I praise Him for all His favors and ask Him for an excess of His bounty and generosity. I testify that there is no deity but Allah alone, there being no associate with Him – the One, the Prevailing, the Generous, the Perpetual Forgiver. And I testify that our master, Muḥammad , is His servant and messenger, His beloved and His pure friend, the best of creatures, the one honored through the mighty Qur'ān [which has been] the continuing miracle over the succession of years and through sunnahs that enlighten the rightly guided – our master, Muḥammad , distinguished for comprehensive speech and ease in religion. May the blessings and peace of Allah be upon him and upon all the prophets and messengers, their families and all righteous people.

To proceed – it has been related to us from `Ali bin Abī Ṭālib, `Abdullāh bin Mas'ūd, Mu'ādh bin Jabal, Abūd-Dardā', Ibn `Umar, Ibn 'Abbās, Anas bin Mālik, Abū Hurayrah and Abū Sa`eed al-Khudri (may Allah be pleased with them) through numerous chains with varied narrations that the Messenger of Allah (ﷺ) said, "Whoever preserves for my nation forty ḥadīths concerning its religion – Allah will resurrect him on the Day of Resurrection among the jurists and scholars." In one narration it says, "...Allah will resurrect him as a jurist and scholar," and in that of Abūd-Dardā', "...I[3] will be for him on the Day of Resurrection an intercessor and a witness." In the narration of Ibn Mas'ūd it says, "...he will be told, 'Enter by any of the doors of Paradise you wish,'" and in that of Ibn `Umar, "...he will be registered among the scholars and resurrected among the martyrs." But ḥadīth scholars have agreed that it is a weak ḥadīth despite its many narrations.

Learned men have compiled within this context countless collections. The first one I have known to do so was `Abdullāh bin al-Mubārak and then Ibn Aslam at-Tūsi, the godly scholar; then al-Ḥasan bin Sufyān an-Nasā'i, Abū Bakr al-Ajurri, Abū Bakr Muḥammad bin Ibrāheem al-Asfahāni, ad-Daraqutni, al-Ḥākim, Abū Nu`aym, Abū `Abdur-Raḥmān as-Sulami, Abū Sa'eed al-Malīni, Abū 'Uthmān as-Sabūni, `Abdullāh bin Muḥammad al-Anṣāri, Abū Bakr al-Bayhaqi and innumerable others from among both previous and later ones.

I have made *istikhārah*[4] to Allah *ta`ālā* concerning the collecting of forty ḥadīths following the example of those outstanding imāms and guardians of Islam. For the

2 The jinn and mankind.

3 i.e., the Prophet (ﷺ).

4 A specific supplication taught by the Prophet (ﷺ) whereby one requests the decision of Allah concerning any ḥalāl undertaking whose benefit or harm is uncertain.

scholars have agreed upon the permissibility of acting on a weak ḥadīth in regard to virtuous deeds. But in spite of this, my reliance is not upon that ḥadīth but rather on his (ﷺ) statement among the authentic ones: "Let the one present among you convey to the absent"[5] and his saying: "May Allah make radiant [the face of] a person who heard my statement and understood it and passed it on as he heard it."[6]

Then there were some scholars who collected forty [ḥadīths] on the fundamentals, while others [did so] on derived matters, others on *jihād,* others on indifference to worldly things, others on conduct, others on speeches, etc., and all of them are sound directions; may Allah be pleased with those who followed them. But I have considered collecting forty more important than all of those, and they would be forty ḥadīths inclusive of all that, but each ḥadīth would be a great precept from those of the religion – one that scholars had described as being the "axis" of Islam or "half" of Islam or "a third" of it or something similar. Furthermore, I would commit myself, regarding these forty, to their being authentic, and most of them are [found] within the two *Ṣaḥeeḥs* of al-Bukhāri and Muslim. I cite them with the chains of narration deleted in order to make their memorization easy and their benefit widespread, *in-sha-Allah ta'ālā.* I then follow up [each of] them with a section defining their more obscure wordings.[7]

Everyone desiring the Hereafter ought to know these ḥadīths for what they contain of important information and because they alert one to all kinds of obedience, which is obvious to whoever reflects upon it. Upon Allah is my dependence, and to Him is my commitment, and [He is] my support. To Him belongs [all] praise and favor, and from Him is [all] success and protection.

---

5 Narrated by aṭ-Ṭabarāni, al-Bukhāri and Muslim.

6 Narrated by Aḥmad and Ibn Mājah – ṣaḥeeḥ.

7 Rather than listing them separately, the definitions have been incorporated into the translation and commentary.

Ḥadīth No. 1

عن أمير المؤمنين أبي حفص عمر بن الخطاب قال: سمعت رسول الله (ﷺ) يقول:

« إِنَّمَا الأَعمَالُ بِالنِّيَّاتِ وَإِنَّمَا لِكُلِّ امرِئٍ مَا نَوَى، فَمَن كَانَت هِجرَتُهُ إِلَى اللهِ وَرَسُولِهِ فَهِجرَتُهُ إِلَى اللهِ وَرَسُولِهِ، وَمَن كَانَت هِجرَتُهُ لِدُنيَا يُصِيبُهَا أَوِ امرَأَةٍ يَنكِحُهَا فَهِجرَتُهُ إِلَى مَا هَاجَرَ إِلَيه»

On the authority of the Commander of the Faithful, Abū Ḥafs, `Umar bin al-Khaṭṭāb, who said: I heard the Messenger of Allah (ﷺ) say:

"Deeds are only by intentions, and every man shall have only what he intended. So one whose hijrah [emigration] was to Allah and His Messenger – his hijrah was to Allah and His Messenger. But one whose hijrah was to achieve a worldly aim or to a woman he would marry – then his hijrah was to that for which he emigrated."

(Narrated by al-Bukhāri and Muslim)

This ḥadīth has been described as the axis of Islam or that about which the religion revolves. Al-Imām Aḥmad observed that the fundamental precepts of Islam are found in three ḥadīths: that of 'Umar: "*Deeds are only by intentions,*" *that of 'Ā'ishah: "Whoever innovates in this matter of ours..."*[1] *and that of an-Nu`mān bin Basheer: "Ḥalāl is clear and ḥarām is clear...*"[2] Al-Bukhāri began his collection with this ḥadīth, almost as if making it an introductory discourse in which he indicates the worthlessness of any deed not done solely for Allah. Muslim placed the ḥadīth at the conclusion of his chapter on *jihād.* Ash-Shāfi'i has said that it is included in seventy subjects of *fiqh* and that it contains a third of knowledge. The reason given by al-Bayhaqi and others is that a servant of Allah earns and acquires benefit through his heart, his tongue and his limbs, the intention being one of the three means.

The *niyyah* (intention), which is primarily in the heart, serves two functions:

1) To define the worship intended – for example, what specific prayer will one be performing at a given time, or whether a *ghusl* (bath) is one required for the lifting of impurity or is *a sunnah,* such as that preceding *iḥrām* for *ḥajj* or *'umrah.*
2) To discern whether the particular act is one of worship – i.e., performed for Allah, or is one of habit, custom or worldly motivation.

Indeed it is the intention, the truth of which is known only to Allah, which distinguishes the righteous deed from that of a hypocrite or one done for a worldly gain. Al-Imām Aḥmad added that the *niyyah* serves to check the self – that one is not doing the deed for anything other than Allah. Numerous sound ḥadīths illustrate the importance of correct intentions and the evil consequences of corrupt ones on the Day of Judgement. But above and beyond the consideration of reward and punishment in the Hereafter is the gratitude to Allah for His countless blessings, both obvious and otherwise, felt by His sincere servant while acknowledging the inadequacy of his own worship. Anxiety

1 Ḥadīth No. 5 of this collection.

2 Ḥadīth No. 6 of this collection.

that his deeds may not be wholly acceptable[3] motivates him toward an excess of work, always seeking the approval of Allah.

The ḥadīth begins with the word "*innamā,*" which is used in Arabic to denote limitation and is usually translated as "is only" or "is but," confirming that which is mentioned while excluding all else. Thus, any work is judged by Allah exclusively on the merit of intention, not on its quantity or apparent greatness. Therefore, it is possible that a seemingly small act done sincerely could be valued by Allah more than a rather conspicuous one and that a sincere servant could gain more reward through his intentions than through works actually accomplished, for the believer's intentions are always better than his deeds, whereas the unbeliever's deeds are better than his intentions.

According to al-Imām an-Nawawi, what is meant by "deeds" (*a`māl*) is deeds of obedience to Allah and not every permissible deed, for those are the means by which a believer aspires to gain His approval. Other commentators have offered that all lawful deeds are included in the generality of the expression. It is understood by students of the language that also included is the concept of validity or acceptability of the deeds in the sight or estimation of Allah (*subḥānahu wa ta'ālā*).

As for the Prophet's saying, "*...and every man shall have only what he intended,*" an additional meaning is derived therefrom – that the deed must be specified, i.e., the person must be aware in his intention of what particular thing he is doing for Allah in order to obtain the reward of that act.

The Messenger of Allah (ﷺ) followed his statement with an example of two types of intentions: one pleasing to Allah and another unacceptable, although the deed itself, emigration, was in all outward appearance the same. Thus, it is perceived as well that there are two categories of *hijrah*: the Islamic one for the cause of the religion and the worldly one for any other purpose, be it *ḥalāl* or *ḥarām*. The original meaning of the word "*hijrah*" is "to leave behind" or "to shun" something. Obligatory emigration to al-Madinah ended with the conquest of Makkah. Other forms of *hijrah* remain preferable, however, for those who are able, such as emigration from lands at war with Islam where Muslims are humiliated or restricted. Included to a lesser degree is emigration from places where unlawful practices or religious innovations prevail or from those where one fears for himself or his property, etc. Leaving behind a life of disobedience is always a religious obligation.

During the period when many of the believers were giving up their families and properties to emigrate to the Prophet (ﷺ) in al-Madinah for the cause of Islam, a man whose aim it was to marry a woman in that city named Umm Qais made the same journey. When the reason for his *hijrah* became evident, he was called "the emigrant of Umm Qais." This was a clear example of a single action for which many worldly motivations were possible as well as the Islamic one. Therefore, it was cited by the Prophet (ﷺ) as a standard by which to measure every deed and the extent of its acceptability to Allah.

---

3 Due to some fault in his attitude such as reluctance, pride or the temptation to make it known to others. Such will not be recognized except by one completely honest with himself.

In answer to the often posed question of whether one may intend something for Allah and for another purpose simultaneously, the following *ḥadīth qudsi* suffices: "*Allah ta'ālā has said, 'I am the most self-sufficient of partners, needing no partnership; so if one does a deed for Me and also for another, then I am disassociated from it, and it is [only] for the [other] partner.'*"[4] Therein is a warning against *shirk*, the association of anything else with Allah. An accepted deed, then, is one pure in intention, done for Him alone, and free of all worldly inducement.

Ibn Rajab, writing on the subject of prejudice, illustrated another subtle difference in intentions: "Here is an unapparent matter which should be brought to attention: An imām might make a plausible statement, having striven to arrive at the truth, his effort rewarded [by Allah] and his error excused. But an avid supporter of his statement might not reach the same degree [of virtue] since perhaps he would not have supported it except for the fact that his imām said it, and if another imām had said it, he would not have accepted it or supported him. So while he imagines he is standing up for the truth, in reality, he is not. While the imām intended to uphold the truth (in spite of possible error), the follower (even though he might be correct) intended only to uphold the word of his leader."[5] The illustration is a warning to scholars as well as ordinary people to continually review their motivations and to be on guard against the continual attempts of Shayṭān to enter the heart, corrupt intentions, and destroy good deeds.

Conversely, a righteous intention accompanying an act or decision that resulted in an unforeseen bad consequence due to circumstances beyond a person's control might absolve him of blame or even bring him reward. This is discussed further under Ḥadīth No. 39.

---

4 Muslim and Ibn Mājah. A *ḥadīth qudsi* (sacred ḥadīth) is a revelation from Allah recounted in the words of the Prophet (ﷺ).

5 *Jāmi' ul-'Ulūm wal-Ḥikam*, pp. 267-268.

Hadīth No. 2

عن عمر أيضا قال:

بَينَمَا نَحنُ جُلُوسٌ عِندَ رَسُولِ اللهِ (ﷺ) ذَاتَ يَومٍ، إذ طَلَعَ عَلَينَا رَجُلٌ شَدِيدُ بَيَاضِ الثِّيَابِ، شَدِيدُ سَوَادِ الشَّعرِ، لاَ يُرَى عَلَيهِ أَثَرُ السَّفَرِ، وَلاَ يَعرِفُهُ مِنَّا أَحَدٌ، حَتَّى جَلَسَ إِلَى النَّبِيِّ (ﷺ)، فَأَسنَدَ رُكبَتَيهِ إِلَى رُكبَتَيهِ، وَوَضَعَ كَفَّيهِ عَلَى فَخِذَيهِ، وَقَالَ: يَا مُحَمَّدُ، أَخبِرنِي عَنِ الإِسلاَمِ. فَقَالَ رَسُولُ اللهِ (ﷺ) «الإِسلاَمُ أَن تَشهَدَ أَن لاَ إِلَهَ إِلاَّ اللهُ وَأَنَّ مُحَمَّدًا رَسُولُ اللهِ، وَتُقِيمَ الصَّلاَةَ، وَتُؤتِيَ الزَّكَاةَ، وَتَصُومَ رَمَضَانَ، وَتَحُجَّ البَيتَ إِن استَطَعتَ إِلَيهِ سَبِيلاً» قَالَ: صَدَقتَ فَعَجِبنَا لَهُ يَسأَلُهُ وَيُصَدِّقُهُ. قَالَ: فَأَخبِرنِي عَنِ الإِيمَانِ. قَالَ: «أَن تُؤمِنَ بِاللهِ، وَمَلاَئِكَتِهِ، وَكُتُبِهِ، وَرُسُلِهِ، وَاليَومِ الآخِرِ، وَتُؤمِنَ بِالقَدَرِ خَيرِهِ وَشَرِّهِ» قَالَ: صَدَقتَ. قَالَ: فَأَخبِرنِي عَنِ الإِحسَانِ. قَالَ: «أَن تَعبُدَ اللهَ كَأَنَّكَ تَرَاهُ، فَإِن لَم تَكُن تَرَاهُ فَإِنَّهُ يَرَاكَ» فَأَخبِرنِي عَنِ السَّاعَةِ. قَالَ: «مَا المَسؤُولُ عَنهَا بِأَعلَمَ مِنَ السَّائِلِ» قَالَ: فَأَخبِرنِي عَن أَمَارَاتِهَا. قَالَ: «أَن تَلِدَ الأَمَةُ رَبَّتَهَا، وَأَن تَرَى الحُفَاةَ العُرَاةَ العَالَةَ رِعَاءَ الشَّاءِ يَتَطَاوَلُونَ فِي البُنيَانِ» ثُمَّ انطَلَقَ فَلَبِثتُ مَلِيًّا ثُمَّ قَالَ: «يَا عُمَرُ أَتَدرِي مَنِ السَّائِلُ؟» قُلتُ: اللهُ وَرَسُولُهُ أَعلَمُ. قَالَ: «فَإِنَّهُ جِبرِيلُ أَتَاكُم يُعَلِّمُكُم دِينَكُم»

Also on the authority of `Umar, who said:

[One day] while we were sitting with the Messenger of Allah (ﷺ), a man came over to us whose clothes were exceedingly white and whose hair was exceedingly black; no signs of travel were seen on him, but none of us knew him. He came and sat down opposite the Prophet (ﷺ) and rested his knees against his, placing the palms of his hands on his thighs. He said, "O Muḥammad , inform me about Islam." The Messenger of Allah (ﷺ) said, "Islam is to testify that there is no god but Allah and that Muḥammad is the Messenger of Allah, to establish prayer, to give zakāh, to fast Ramadhān, and to make the pilgrimage to the House[6] if you are able to do so." He said, "You have spoken the truth," and we wondered at his asking him and confirming it. He said, "Then inform me about īmān."[7] He said, "It is to believe in Allah, His angels, His books, His messengers, and the Last Day, and to believe in predestination, both the good and the evil thereof." He said, "You have spoken the truth." He said, "Then inform me about iḥsān."[8] He said, "It is to worship Allah as though you see Him; if you do not see Him, indeed, He sees you." He said, "Then inform me about the Hour."[9] He said, "The one questioned about it knows no more than the questioner." He said, "Then inform me of its signs." He said, "That the slave-woman will give birth to her mistress and that you will see barefooted, naked, destitute shepherds competing in the loftiness of constructions." Then he departed, and I stayed for a time. Then he said, "O `Umar, do you know who the questioner was?" I said, "Allah and His Messenger are more knowing." He said, "It was Gabriel. He came to you to teach you your religion."

(Narrated by Muslim)

6 The Ka`bah in Makkah.
7 Faith, belief.
8 Good conduct, proficiency in religion.
9 The time of resurrection.

This ḥadīth contains a comprehensive description of the religion, which is comprised of the three concepts of "*islām*," *īmān*" and "*iḥsān*." For this reason the Prophet (ﷺ) said in conclusion, "That was Gabriel who came to teach you your religion." The ḥadīth has been called "Umm us-Sunnah"[10] just as Sūrah al-Fātiḥah is called "Umm al-Qur'ān." Within it are included all categories of good deeds, both apparent and unapparent, and from it are derived the sciences of *Sharī'ah.*

The Prophet (ﷺ) and his companions were gathered, as they often did, to discuss matters of religion. Gabriel's approach did not cause any particular excitement since he appeared in the form of a man and thus was assumed to be one. All that was noted as unusual was his immaculate appearance, whereas the effects of a long journey should have been discernible on a newly arrived stranger. As he began to question the Prophet (ﷺ), they also found it strange that he approved each answer given, as if he had a previous knowledge of the matter, while this knowledge could only be obtained, as far as they knew, from the Prophet himself. As this person seemed to be an examiner rather than an ordinary inquirer, their attention sharpened. Thus, it was insured that the lesson would be well retained by all those present.

In defining the pillars of each of the three concepts, it becomes evident that although the terms "*islām*" and *īmān*" are often used interchangeably, each of them is separate and distinct in itself. The Prophet (ﷺ) describes "*islām*" here as the execution of Allah's ordinances, at least outwardly. "*Imān,*" on the other hand, is correct and complete inner belief, which, as all of the *ṣaḥābah* agreed, is necessarily proven by certain actions. So both include deeds; however, those of a *mu'min* (true believer) supersede those of a Muslim. Hence, every *mu'min* is a Muslim, but not every Muslim is a *mu'min.*

Besides the five pillars named here, "*islām*" includes such visible actions as showing good manners, honesty in dealings, refraining from harmful behavior, advising others, etc. But such deeds may be performed for reasons other than faith – by hypocrites, for example, or by people who merely desire to be accepted within the society. Thus, Allah (*subḥānahu wa ta'ālā*) clarified the difference between "*islām*" and *īmān*" in verses 14 and 15 of *Sūrah al-Ḥujurāt,* correcting those who had claimed faith prematurely. Among the actions and reactions induced by *īmān* are preference of Allah and His Messenger (ﷺ) over every worldly matter, loving and hating others only for the cause of Allah, giving or withholding for His cause, directing all of one's efforts toward the approval of Allah, happiness at having done some good and sadness and remorse at having done something wrong, giving preference to other believers over oneself, concern about and aiding those in need, attentiveness at the mention of Allah and upon hearing the Qur'ān, reliance upon Allah in all affairs, satisfaction with what Allah has decreed, preference of worldly hardships over returning to disbelief, etc.

We have noted that *islām,* or outward submission, is the minimum degree entitling one by law to the rights of a Muslim. Then Allah will reward such a person according to his deeds and intentions. Higher in rank and preferable to Allah is the *mu'min* – the Muslim who has true faith in all that listed in the ḥadīth:

---

10 The "mother," i.e., foundation of the sunnah.

1) belief in Allah – i.e., in His existence, His perfect and absolute attributes, His superiority over all creation, and that there is nothing similar to Him
2) belief in His angels – noble creatures created from light who have no free will but execute the commands of Allah and worship Him continuously
3) belief in His books – Allah revealed scriptures[11] to certain of His messengers, and He revealed the Qur'ān as the final message to mankind
4) belief in His messengers – that they were truthful in what they conveyed about Allah, that they were supported by Him with miracles, and that they faithfully delivered His messages to the people
5) belief in the Last Day, i.e., the Day of Resurrection and what was revealed concerning it: destruction of the present universe, renewed creation, emergence from the graves, the Gathering, the Judgement, Paradise and Hellfire, etc.
6) belief in *al-qadar* (predestination), i.e., in Allah's knowledge of all that is to be and in the fact that He (*subḥānahu wa ta'ālā*) has originated and is the primary cause of all things and occurrences. Al-Imām an-Nawawi has mentioned four kinds of *qadar*:
   a. Allah's knowledge and decree which have always existed, having had no beginning
   b. His decree registered in *al-Lawḥ al-Maḥfūth*[12] which is subject to change, as He says in the Qur'ān:

   يَمْحُوا اللهُ مَا يَشَاءُ وَيُثْبِتُ

   "Allah eliminates what He wills or affirms."[13]

   c. What is decreed while one is in the womb and recorded by an angel[14]
   d. What is decreed while another decree is approaching its time and place, such as when a disaster is prevented or lessened through the mercy of Allah or because of supplication[15]

The third and highest degree of religion is that of *iḥsān*. The Prophet's description, worshipping Allah "as if you see Him" with the reminder that "He sees you," alludes to worship accompanied by an acute consciousness of Allah which leads to sincerity and precision in deeds. In reality, *iḥsān* is that which perfects every deed of both *islām* and *īmān*. It is reflected in a willingness to do more than one's duty and being satisfied with less than one's right while seeking the acceptance of Allah. In this way everyday dealings with others become acts of worship and are rewarded as such. *Iḥsān* is an outward expression of *taqwā*[16] and awareness of the Creator's all-pervading knowledge.

---

11 Although their original forms have not been preserved. No number is given, but they include those sent down to Ibrāheem, Mūsā, Dāwūd and 'Isā (peace be upon them).

12 The "Preserved Slate," which is with Allah (*subhanahu wa ta`ala*) in which all things are recorded.

13 Sūrah ar-Ra'd, 13:39.

14 See Ḥadīth No. 4.

15 In a ḥadīth graded as ḥasan (accepted), the Prophet (ﷺ) said, "*Nothing repels decree except supplication.*" (Narrated by at-Tirmidhi and al-Ḥākim)

16 i.e., inner piety, love and fear of Allah, and caution in order to avoid displeasing Him.

The request, "Inform me about the Hour," and the answer given bring attention to the fact that this is information which Allah (*subḥānahu wa ta'ālā*) has kept to Himself, dispelling any speculation that prophets, angels or any other creatures possess knowledge of its time. Therefore, any who make claims to that effect testify to their own untruthfulness. Additionally, it is shown from the Prophet's example that there is nothing shameful in admitting that one does not know a particular answer when asked; on the contrary, it is an obligation to do so.

"Then inform me of its signs" implies that certain conditions will precede the time of resurrection which will be recognized by people on earth. Although the signs enumerated in various other ḥadīth*s* are many, on this occasion the Prophet (ﷺ) mentioned only two. The first of these is that the slave-woman will give birth to her mistress.[17] Among the interpretations given are

1) that there will be conquests resulting in a great number of war captives whose children born to the conquerors will be nobles through the lineage of their fathers
2) that ignorance of the law will become widespread so that masters will sell those slaves who have born them children;[18] then after a time, a daughter (or son) might unknowingly purchase her mother from the slave market
3) that slaves will give birth to future kings
4) that disrespect for parents will reach the point where children treat their mothers as if they were slaves – insulting and humiliating them.

As for the second sign, certain conclusions are drawn from it as well:

1) The weakest and poorest class of people will become rich, ostentatious, and dominant in the land
2) Unqualified people will become rulers and occupy positions of responsibility – In another ḥadīth the Prophet (ﷺ) stated that among the signs of the Hour is the disappearance of knowledge and spread of ignorance.[19] Ignorant rulers will then corrupt the religion and the world, denying people their rights and taking over their properties. In the prevailing corruption all conditions will be reversed: the liar will be believed while the truthful is denied; the traitor will be entrusted while the trustworthy is considered a traitor; the ignorant will speak while the knowledgeable will remain silent – or will be eliminated altogether, as the Prophet (ﷺ) explained: "*Knowledge will be taken away by the scholars being taken [in death].*"[20]

'Umar, who related the ḥadīth, continued with the observation that he remained with the other companions for some time after the departure of the stranger, whereupon they were informed by the Prophet (ﷺ) that the questioner was none but the angel Gabriel who had come for the purpose of instructing them. Thus, it is shown as well that a lesson may be emphasized by the use of varied teaching methods, among them the posing of questions to students.

---

17 Scholars have pointed out that the male gender (i.e., master) is understood to be included as well.

18 Which is unlawful for them to do according to the Shaīi'ah.

19 Narrated by al-Bukhāri and Muslim.

20 Narrated by al-Bukhāri and Muslim.

Hadīth No. 3

عن أبي عبد الرحمن عبد الله بن عمر بن الخطاب قال: سمعت رسول الله (ﷺ) يقول:

«بُنِيَ الإِسْلَامُ عَلَى خَمْسٍ: شَهَادَةِ أَنْ لاَ إِلَهَ إِلاَّ اللهُ، وَإِقَامِ الصَّلَاةِ، وَإِيتَاءِ الزَّكَاةِ، وَحَجِّ البَيْتِ، وَصَوْمِ رَمَضَانَ»

On the authority of Abū ʿAbdur-Raḥmān, ʿAbdullāh, son of ʿUmar bin al-Khaṭṭāb, who said: I heard the Messenger of Allah (ﷺ) say:

"Islam has been built on five: testifying that there is no deity but Allah and that Muḥammad is the Messenger of Allah, the establishment of prayer, giving zakāh, making the pilgrimage to the House, and fasting Ramadhān."

(Narrated by al-Bukhāri and Muslim)

The pillars of Islam were enumerated in the previous ḥadīth in comparison with those of īmān in order to define and distinguish each. This ḥadīth presents them in another light. What is emphasized here is that these five "pillars," as they have been called, are indeed the basis of Islam without which the religion cannot stand, just as a building cannot stand without strong supports rooted in a foundation. This does not mean, however, that Islam is limited to these five – far from it. For obedience in everything that Allah has ordained is included in Islam and is, in fact, essential for its completion and perfection. Every Muslim will be judged in the Hereafter according to his efforts to obey every order and avoid every prohibition.

What is meant here is simply that all of the other obligations are what completes Islam and makes it good (for what use is a building without walls, a roof, doors and windows, interior furnishings, etc.?), while the main pillars are the minimum that can be called "Islam." Hence, the Prophet (ﷺ) did not say that these five pillars are Islam but that Islam is built upon them; i.e., they must be present before Islam can be completed. And since, as noted previously, the deeds of Islam are principally actions which are observable (those of the tongue and the body), a person is considered a Muslim as long as the basic "pillars" are present.

The first of them is *shahādah*, or testimony that there is no deity, i.e., nothing worthy of worship except Allah (*subḥānahu wa taʿālā*) and that Muḥammad (ﷺ) is His messenger, i.e., the spokesman for Allah by His authority. For this reason Allah, in the Qurʾān, has made obedience to the Prophet (ﷺ) incumbent on all Muslims. Testifying requires that one be truthful and sincere, and it includes two aspects:

1) recognition and admission within the self
2) bearing witness of the fact before others, i.e., asserting one's conviction, which is then proven by his fulfillment of the other four requirements

"No deity but Allah" involves the question of divine authority – submission and willing acceptance of the Creator's right to govern creation. *Shahādah* is obviously the first building block of Islam without which there can be no Islam.

Scholars' views differ over the remaining four pillars – whether or not the omission of one of them removes one from the ranks of Muslims. It is generally conceded that disobedience or neglect with admission of sin does not do so but that the outright denial of an Islamic obligation or a prohibition given by Allah in the Qur'ān amounts to refusal of His rightful authority and is thus seen as *kufr* (disbelief).

The second pillar has not been stated as "prayer" but as "the establishment of prayer" at its proper times and according to its specified conditions.[21] It is the faithful performance of this duty correctly to the best of one's ability with presence of mind and humble awareness of his position before his Creator without neglect or postponement of the obligatory prayers. Several authentic ḥadīths have equated the deliberate abandonment of prayer with reversion to unbelief.

Zakāh (the required yearly expenditure from excess wealth) has been mentioned in conjunction with *ṣalāh* (prayer) in 26 verses of the Qur'ān. Thus, after the death of the Prophet (ﷺ), Abū Bakr, with the support of `Umar and the other *ṣahābah* (may Allah be pleased with them), refused to allow any who called themselves Muslims to refrain from giving *zakāh* on the pretext that it was due only to the Messenger of Allah (ﷺ).

Ḥajj (pilgrimage) is obligatory but once in a lifetime for those who have the physical and financial ability. In the Qur'ān[22] Allah has described refusal of this obligation as disbelief, and He (*subḥānahu wa ta'ālā*) is fully aware as to whether a person is truly unable or merely unwilling. Fasting the month of Ramadhān, which precedes *ḥajj* in other ḥadīths, also stipulates physical ability and postponement of fasting is permitted on days of inability or hardship.

Although *jihād* in the sense of armed struggle was commended by the Prophet (ﷺ) as the peak of Islam and the best of deeds, it has been pointed out that it is not among its pillars due to the fact that it is not an obligation upon every single Muslim (unless there is an invasion of his territory) but rather upon specific groups at various times and according to circumstances. Other forms of *jihād*, such as *da`wah* work, are, in reality, practiced by those who have reached the level of *īmān.*

21 As laid out in the Prophet's sunnah.

22 See Sūrah Aali 'Imrān, 3:97.

Ḥadīth No. 4

عن أبي عبد الرحمن عبد الله بن مسعود قال: حدثنا رسول الله (ﷺ) وهو الصادق المصدوق:

«إِنَّ أَحَدَكُم يُجمَعُ خَلقُهُ فِي بَطنِ أُمِّهِ أَربَعِينَ يَومًا نُطفَةً، ثُمَّ يَكُونُ عَلَقَةً مِثلَ ذٰلِك، ثُمَّ يَكُونُ مُضغَةً مِثلَ ذٰلِكَ، ثُمَّ يُرسَلُ إِلَيهِ المَلَكُ فَيَنفُخُ فِيهِ الرُّوحَ وَيُؤمَرُ بِأَربَعِ كَلِمَاتٍ: بِكَتبِ رِزقِهِ، وَأَجَلِهِ، وَعَمَلِهِ، وَشَقِيٌّ أَو سَعِيدٌ. فَوَاللهِ الَّذِي لاَ إِلٰهَ غَيرُهُ إِنَّ أَحَدَكُم لَيَعمَلُ بِعَمَلِ أَهلِ الجَنَّةِ، حَتَّى مَا يَكُونَ بَينَهُ وَبَينَهَا إِلاَّ ذِرَاعٌ، فَيَسبِقُ عَلَيهِ الكِتَابُ فَيَعمَلُ بِعَمَلِ أَهلِ النَّارِ فَيَدخُلُهَا. وَإِنَّ أَحَدَكُم لَيَعمَلُ بِعَمَلِ أَهلِ النَّارِ، حَتَّى مَا يَكُونَ بَينَهُ وَبَينَهَا إِلاَّ ذِرَاعٌ، فَيَسبِقُ عَلَيهِ الكِتَابُ فَيَعمَلُ بِعَمَلِ أَهلِ الجَنَّةِ فَيَدخُلُهَا»

On the authority of Abū 'Abdur-Raḥmān, 'Abdullāh bin Mas'ūd, who said: The Messenger of Allah (ﷺ), and he is the truthful, the believed,[23] narrated to us:

"Indeed, the creation of one of you is brought together in his mother's belly for forty days in the form of a zygote, then he is a clinging clot for a like period, then a morsel of flesh for a like period, then there is sent to him the angel who blows the [human] soul into him and is commanded about four matters:[24] to write down his provision, his life span, his actions, and [whether he will be] unhappy or happy. And by Allah, other than whom there is no deity, indeed, one of you does the deeds of the people of Paradise until there is not between him and it except an arm's length, but the decree overtakes him so he does the deeds of the people of the Fire and enters it. And indeed, one of you does the deeds of the people of the Fire until there is not between him and it except an arm's length, but the decree overtakes him so he does the deeds of the people of Paradise and enters it."

(Narrated by al-Bukhāri and Muslim)

This ḥadīth deals with the condition of man from beginning to end and his states from before his entrance into the world to after his departure from it. It also confirms the concept of *qadar* (decree or predestination).

The first stages of development mentioned correspond to those given in the Qur'ān. The bringing together or gathering of one's creation in his mother's belly may refer to the combining of the male and female substance within the womb or to the formation of the embryo; however, most scholars prefer the view that although its beginnings may be observed in the second stage, the actual formation takes place during the third stage of development when the fetus resembles a "chewed lump of flesh."[25] At the end of the three 40 day periods, i.e., after about four months, a human soul is bestowed upon the fetus through an angel who has the additional duty of recording what Allah (*subḥānahu wa ta'ālā*) has predestined for that individual.[26]

---

23 Believed as to what came to him (ﷺ) of divine revelation.

24 Literally, "words."

25 For a detailed study, see *Introduction to Embryology* by Dr. Keith Moore (1988).

26 Although some scholars have permitted a woman to abort an embryo before it is endowed with the human soul, others reject this view, stating that it remains a crime against a living being that has already been conceived and possibly formed and cannot be compared to preventative measures where a child has not been conceived.

Specifically, four aspects are recorded concerning his destiny:

1) His provision (*rizq*), i.e., the extent of his share or allotted portion of sustenance and other blessings from Allah, both material and otherwise
2) His life span (*ajal*), i.e., the extent of his appointed term upon the earth or the time of his death
3) His deeds (*`amal*), or more literally, work, or those deliberate actions in which intention is involved
4) The result or outcome of his life – whether he will ultimately be prosperous, blessed and in a state of well-being or unprosperous, distressed and in a state of adversity

The ḥadīth states that the final and permanent condition of every person is predestined and that it is the consequence of his deeds. `Ali bin Abī Ṭālib reported that the Prophet (ﷺ) said, "*There is no soul given life but that Allah has decreed its place in Paradise or Hellfire and decreed that it will be unhappy or happy.*" A man said, "O Messenger of Allah, should we not then leave it to our decree and cease working?" He (ﷺ) replied, "*Work, for everyone is disposed toward that for which he was created. As for the people of happiness, they are disposed toward the deeds of the people of happiness, but as for the people of unhappiness, they are disposed toward the deeds of the people of unhappiness.*" Then he recited verses 5 through 10 of *Sūrah al-Layl.*[27]

Therefore, one should not submit passively to what he supposes to be his fate, for he has no knowledge of that. Nor should he surrender to adverse situations, for numerous ḥadīths prohibit such behavior. Rather, every effort is obligatory upon the believer to make the best of each situation and avoid harm to the best of his ability, whether in this world or the Hereafter, and Allah (*subḥānahu wa ta`ālā*) will hold him responsible on the Day of Judgement for negligence to do so.

The latter part of the ḥadīth emphasizes the importance of one's final deeds. Several other traditions state that deeds are judged according to how they are sealed, i.e., concluded. An important precept derived from this is that one cannot judge by outer appearance whether any person is among those destined for Paradise or those destined for Hell, as in the Prophet's saying, "*You must not be impressed by anyone until you observe that by which his life is sealed...*"[28] This is so because the destiny decreed by Allah is concealed from the knowledge of mankind, whereas a person's deeds and actions are often visible. So although one might possibly be deceived by the deeds of a hypocrite, for example, his final deed will often expose the reality of his intention. Another ḥadīth illustrates:

During a particular encounter with the polytheists, a man among the Prophet's companions showed great enthusiasm in pursuing and striking the enemy soldiers – so much so that they remarked, "No one fulfilled his duty today as much as he did." But the Messenger of Allah (ﷺ) observed, "*He is among the people of Hellfire.*" Someone among them said, "I am his friend, so I will follow [i.e., observe] him." Then the man in question was severely injured, and he became impatient for death. He braced the handle of his sword against the ground with the point between his breasts and threw

---

27 Narrated by al-Bukhāri and Muslim.

28 Narrated by Aḥmad – *ṣaḥeeḥ*.

himself upon it, killing himself. The man [who had seen him] returned to the Prophet (ﷺ) and said, "I bear witness that you are the messenger of Allah" and related what had occurred. The Prophet (ﷺ) said, "*Indeed, a man may do the work of the inhabitants of Paradise – as it appears to the people – while he is from the inhabitants of the Fire; and a man may do the work of the inhabitants of the Fire – as it appears to the people – while he is from the inhabitants of Paradise.*"[29]

Perhaps the key to this issue is in the words "as it appears to the people," for only Allah knows the true motivations. The words are explicit in indicating that those deeds referred to in the ḥadīth are in reality not as they are presumed to be. What appears to be righteousness and piety could possibly be a great amount of deeds invalidated in the sight of Allah by the person's seeking of worldly recognition and praise instead of His acceptance. And what appears as sinful may not be so in particular circumstances, as illustrated by the story of Prophet Mūsā and al-Khidhr.[30]

If, on the other hand, it is assumed that the deeds mentioned in this particular ḥadīth are actually as described, then further conclusions can be drawn. Since it is most unusual for a person to change abruptly at the end of his life, the ḥadīth states a mere possibility and not a general rule. Further, it has been repeatedly observed that among these few cases, those who repent and correct themselves in their last days far outnumber those who suddenly turn to evil, indicating Allah's great generosity in His acceptance and forgiveness of such individuals even after a lifetime of ingratitude and wrongdoing.

Since ending a good life with an evil deed remains a possibility, however remote, the believer is warned against complacency and the temptation to rely on past deeds for salvation. He is advised to continually check his intentions and continue his efforts toward righteousness up until his last breath as long as his mental facilities are intact in order to seal his lifetime of work with goodness and earn the approval of his Lord, who will assist him in what he intends.

Allah, the Just and Merciful, has provided mankind with guidance and has willed to give him a free choice within certain capabilities. He (*subḥānahu wa ta'ālā*) will not take man to account except for that within his control and only to the extent of his ability. The decision, by Allah's will, belongs to every individual who will eventually reap the fruits of his choice. And thus, by Allah's will, every man is responsible for his own ultimate destiny.

---

29 Narrated by al-Bukhāri and Muslim.

30 See Sūrah al-Kahf, 18:60-82.

Ḥadīth No. 5

عن أم المؤمنين أم عبد الله عائشة قالت: قال رسول الله (ﷺ):

« مَن أحدَثَ فِي أمرِنَا هَذَا مَا لَيسَ مَنهُ فَهُوَ رَدٌّ»

رواه البخاري ومسلم وفي رواية لمسلم: « مَن عَمِلَ عَمَلاً لَيسَ عَلَيهِ أمرُنَا فَهُوَ رَدٌّ»

On the authority of the Mother of the Believers, Umm `Abdullāh, 'Ā'ishah, who said: The Messenger of Allah (ﷺ) said:

"He who innovates something in this matter of ours that is not a part of it – it will be rejected."

(Narrated by al-Bukhāri and Muslim)

In one version by Muslim it says:

"He who does a deed not in accordance with our matter – it will be rejected."

Here is one of the comprehensive statements of the Prophet (ﷺ) which is a basis for several fundamental principles. It provides a criterion for evaluation of the visible aspects of one's deeds, complementing the ḥadīth, "Deeds are only by intention," which deals with the unapparent aspect. Combining the import of both, scholars have concluded that there are two conditions for the acceptability of any deed by Allah (*subḥānahu wa ta`ālā*): sincerity of intention (*ikhlās*), i.e., it must be done for Allah alone, and correctness (*ṣawāb*), i.e., it must be done in the way ordained by Him in the Qur'ān and sunnah of the Prophet (ﷺ).

The ḥadīth warns against innovation (*bid'ah*)[31] in all matters of religion. In this context the word "matter" (*amr*) carries the meaning of religious practice and law. "Rejected" means that the deed is unacceptable to Allah and so will not be rewarded. It is a clear prohibition against making any changes in or additions to the religion and warns those sects differing with *Ahl as-Sunnah* of their error, for anything claimed to be a valid religious practice must be based upon a proof from the Qur'ān or the sunnah. That is because Allah (*subḥānahu wa ta'ālā*) has completed and perfected the religion (Islam) which He ordained for mankind as stated in Sūrah al-Mā'idah,[32] and He has not omitted from it anything beneficial to man. One who asserts otherwise by insistence on some alternative way places himself in danger of falling into disbelief through his contradiction of the Qur'ān and refusal of obedience to the Prophet (ﷺ). The Messenger of Allah (ﷺ) elaborated further when he said, "*Indeed, the best statement is the Book of Allah, and the best guidance is the guidance of Muḥammad (ﷺ). And the worst of matters are the newly devised ones, and every innovation is misguidance.*"[33] Again, this refers to matters of religion and not those of worldly life.

The deeds to be assessed by this criterion fall into two categories: those of individual worship, which have been specified and precisely defined by Allah and His

---

31 For an explanation of the term, see Ḥadīth No. 28.

32 Sūrah al-Mā'idah, 5:3.

33 Narrated by Muslim.

Messenger (ﷺ), and those relating to dealings with one's fellow human beings. Within the latter category, all legal rulings, whether issued for the public interest or concerning individual parties, must have their foundations in and be in compliance with the divine *sharī'ah.*[34] Moreover, those instructions, written contracts, verbal agreements, etc. expressly forbidden therein are not to be honored, and any benefits or profits obtained through them are unlawful.

This ḥadīth is one which should be memorized, made known to the people, and employed for the prevention of every kind of wrongdoing. For although many are aware of the specific prohibitions[35] stated in the Qur'ān and ḥadīth literature, far fewer people give attention to deviations in the more private sphere of worship, particularly when an ignorant majority has been led by custom or by some popular "shaykh" to believe that certain innovations are good and are valid methods for seeking nearness to Allah. These innovations are either practices that have no basis in the *sunnah* whatsoever or those prescribed therein but performed in a way or for a reason contrary to that prescribed, thereby blemishing a deed which otherwise would have been commendable.[36] Awareness is the first step to amendment.

Any act performed with the sincere intention of drawing nearer to Allah must first be one ordained by Him, either through His Book or through His Prophet (ﷺ). Then it must be done correctly: precisely in the way demonstrated or instructed by the Messenger of Allah (ﷺ), who was sent to mankind with complete guidance in all matters of faith and its application to the affairs of human life.

---

34 Such rulings, in contrast to blameworthy innovations, are not ends in themselves but provide means to assist people in carrying out a prescribed obligation or avoiding harm.

35 Such as those concerning usury, intoxicants, unlawful sexual relations, etc.

36 To cite one example: insistence on the superiority of fasting on a particular day not indicated in the Prophet's sunnah (although any day of fasting would normally have merit without an erroneous assertion attached to it).

Hadīth No. 6

عن أبي عبد الله النعمان بن بشير قال: سمعت رسول الله (ﷺ) يقول:

«إِنَّ الحَلاَلَ بَيِّنٌ، وَإِنَّ الحَرَامَ بَيِّنٌ، وَبَينَهُمَا أُمورٌ مُشْتَبِهَاتٌ لاَ يَعلَمُهُنَّ كَثِيرٌ مِنَ النَّاسِ. فَمَن اتَّقَى الشُّبُهَاتِ فَقَد استَبرَأَ لِدِينِهِ وَعِرضِهِ. وَمَن وَقَعَ فِي الشُّبُهَاتِ وَقَعَ فِي الحَرَامِ، كَالرَّاعِي يَرعَى حَولَ الحِمَى يُوشِكُ أَن يَرتَعَ فِيهِ. أَلاَ وَإِنَّ لِكُلِّ مَلِكٍ حِمًى، أَلاَ وَإِنَّ حِمَى اللهِ مَحَارِمُهُ. أَلاَ وَإِنَّ فِي الجَسَدِ مُضغَةً، إِذَا صَلَحَت صَلَحَ الجَسَدُ كُلُّهُ، وَإِذَا فَسَدَت فَسَدَ الجَسَدُ كُلُّهُ، أَلاَ وَهِيَ القَلبُ»

On the authority of Abū `Abdullāh, an-Nu'mān bin Basheer, who said: I heard the Messenger of Allah (ﷺ) say:

"The lawful is clear, and the unlawful is clear, and between the two of them are doubtful matters about which many people do not know. So he who avoids doubtful matters has sought to clear himself in regard to his religion and his honor, but he who falls into doubtful matters [then] falls into the unlawful, like the shepherd who pastures around a private area, all but grazing therein. Undoubtedly, every sovereign has private property, and indeed, the private property of Allah is His prohibited matters. Undoubtedly, within the body is a morsel of flesh which, when it is good, the whole body is good; but when it is corrupt, the whole body is corrupt. Indeed, it is the heart."

(Narrated by al-Bukhāri and Muslim)

The ḥadīth presents certain facts and a directive that is fundamental to the religion. First, the Prophet (ﷺ) confirmed that what is purely *ḥalāl* (lawful) is recognized, and what is purely *ḥarām* (unlawful) has been mentioned distinctly by Allah, either in the Qur'ān or through His Messenger (ﷺ). As He stated: يُبَيِّنُ اللهُ لَكُم أَن تَضِلُّوا ***"Allah makes clear to you [His law] lest you go astray."***[37] These rulings are not subject to doubt and are generally known. But other matters are not widely known by the people or even agreed upon by the scholars, having been subject to differing interpretations and opinions. These "doubtful matters," however, are not doubtful in the absolute sense, as shown by the words "which many people do not know." Thus, it is understood that there are some scholars who do know the truth about each of these matters and that their reasoning is correct.

For those who are uncertain, either due to doubtful evidence or confusion about whether or not a ruling applies to a particular situation, the Prophet (ﷺ) advised prudence and caution, which is the essence of *taqwā,*[38] pointing out that it is preferable to avoid that whose permissibility is doubtful. Two reasons are cited by scholars: First, that the matter in doubt could be a means leading to what is clearly *ḥarām,* so that the person, when indulging himself, gradually lets down his guard and drifts into what is beyond doubt. And second, that one who embarks on what is doubtful to him might possibly be doing that which is actually unlawful and has been declared so by those who are knowledgeable about the matter.[39] Thus, whoever avoids a matter about which

---

37 Sūrah an-Nisaa', 4:176.

38 See footnote no. 16 to Ḥadīth No. 2.

39 There are some who deliberately avoid religious knowledge, assuming that one cannot be held responsible for what he does not know, while in reality, wherever such knowledge is obtainable, →

he has misgivings has sought to clear himself, i.e., he has made an effort to earn the approval of Allah, so Allah will be pleased with him in regard to his religion. As for clearing his honor, it means that he will not have given anyone an opportunity to doubt him, think ill of him, or criticize his action.

A person who is careless about falling into doubtful matters has been compared to a shepherd who allows his flock to approach a plot of land whose owner has warned of the consequences of trespassing. How can he possibly prevent his animals from breaking into that plot, especially when they are lured by green grass and lush vegetation? Hence, scholars have ruled that whatever might lead to *ḥarām* is also *ḥarām,* such as the improper dress and behavior that could possibly lead to an unlawful sexual relationship or the production, sale, purchase and serving of intoxicants, the consumption of which is *ḥarām.* The principle of a danger zone is thus established to protect the Muslim against the whisperings of Shayṭān and of his own soul.

"Every sovereign" may mean a king or an owner. It is known that some among the Arabs used to designate for themselves and mark off a portion of land, issuing a public threat to punish or fight anyone who dared to cross into it. Allah (*subḥānahu wa ta'ālā*) has issued warnings to those who would violate His injunctions and made clear the grievous consequences in the Hereafter if not in this life as well.

The Prophet (ﷺ) was aware that this directive of his would only be observed by those who revere Allah and fear His displeasure. Therefore, he tied it to the mention of the heart, as he said on another occasion, "*Taqwā is here,*" pointing to his chest.[40] The ḥadīth shows that behavior is dependent upon the state of the heart, which is sometimes compared to a king who commands his subjects (i.e., the rest of the body). So when the heart is sound, the body will do good deeds, avoid prohibited ones, and even avoid those subject to doubt. But when the heart is corrupted and ruled by worldly desires, the body will not resist temptation and will be led into disobedience, easily convinced by numerous excuses, among them, ignorance.

ignorance is neither justified nor excused.

40 See Ḥadīth No. 35.

Hadīth No. 7

عن أبي رقية تميم بن أوس الداري أن النبي (ﷺ) قال:

«الدِّينُ النَّصِيحَةُ» قُلْنَا: لِمَنْ؟ قَالَ: «لِلهِ، وَلِكِتَابِهِ، وَلِرَسُولِهِ، وَلأَئِمَّةِ المُسلِمِينَ وَعَامَّتِهِم»

On the authority of Abū Ruqayyah, Tameem bin Aus ad-Dāri, that the Prophet (ﷺ) said:

"Religion is sincerity."[41] We said, "To whom?" He said, "To Allah and to His Book, to His Messenger, and to the leaders of Muslims and their common people."

(Narrated by Muslim)

"Religion is sincerity" has been interpreted by some to mean that they are one in the same, i.e., that sincerity, as described in this ḥadīth, may be called religion. But the consensus among scholars is that it is like the Prophet's statement, "*The ḥajj is `Arafah*," meaning that the latter is the larger or most important part of the former. The following examples have been given for the various forms of sincerity mentioned by Allah's Messenger (ﷺ):

1) To Allah (*subḥānahu wa ta'ālā*): Belief in Him, rejection of *shirk*[42] and of distortions concerning His attributes, describing Him with all the attributes of perfection and majesty and disassociating Him from any imperfection or similarity to His creation, obedience to Him and avoidance of disobedience, striving against those who oppose belief in Him or advocate *shirk,* loving because of Him and hating because of Him, recognition of and gratitude for His favors, purity of intention in every matter, inviting others to all of the aforementioned and encouraging it while being courteous to all people.[43]

2) To His Book: Belief that the revealed words of Allah have no resemblance to the words of men and that none of creation can produce anything similar, belief in all that the Qur'ān contains, holding it in esteem, reciting it with true recitation, beautifully and with reverence, pronouncing each letter correctly, defending it against deviant interpretations and the abuse of attackers, understanding its information and examples, learning from its perspectives, contemplating its wonders, acting according to what is specific therein and accepting what is unspecific, being occupied in the study of its laws – its general rulings and its particular ones and what abrogates and is abrogated thereof, spreading knowledge of its sciences and inviting others to it and to all of the aforementioned.

3) To His Messenger (ﷺ): Belief in his message (the Qur'ān) and in all he brought (the sunnah), obedience in what he ordered and prohibited, love and respect for him, animosity toward his enemies and support of his supporters, recognition of his right, adherence to his morals and manners, love for his family and companions, perpetuation of his sunnah and opposition to those who introduce innovations into

---

41 Sincerity in advice, counsel and conduct; desiring the best for the other party.

42 The association in worship or obedience of anything with Allah.

43 In reality, the benefit of all this is to the person himself, since Allah is not in need of his sincerity, but He rewards for every good deed.

the religion, propagation of his message and of his sunnah while refuting false allegations about it – respect for its scholars, pursuit of its sciences and comprehension of its meanings while refraining from speaking without knowledge, inviting others to it and teaching it in a gentle manner.

4) To the leaders of Muslims: Aiding them in what is right and obedience to them therein, cautioning them and reminding them politely, informing them about that of which they are unaware concerning the rights of the people while encouraging the latter to obey their rulers,[44] joining them in *jihad,* praying behind them, preventing them from being deluded by false praise, not taking up arms against them if they show prejudice, injustice or bad conduct but practicing patience and advising them when possible and supplicating for their righteousness and reform.

5) To the Muslim people: Guiding them toward their best interests in this world and the Hereafter and helping them to achieve them, covering up their faults and shortcomings, defending them from harm and procuring for them benefit, enjoining upon them what is right and forbidding what is wrong – gently and with pure intention, compassion for them, respect for their elderly and mercy towards their young, giving good advice, refraining from cheating or envying them, liking for them what one would like for himself, defending their properties and honor by word and deed, and encouraging them to practice all of the aforementioned.

Sincere advice is among the collective duties of Islam (*fardh kifāyah*). If a sufficient number of qualified people perform this duty, the others are absolved. However, if an insufficient number do so, the entire community is held accountable. Conditions cited by scholars for capability are full knowledge of the matter in question, a degree of influence over those advised, discretion as to the method of advice, and reasonable security from negative repercussions, i.e., reactions that would cause the situation to worsen, not merely hostility toward the advisor. So when a Muslim knows that his counsel will be accepted and his advice heeded and he will not harm or be harmed, then that is obligatory upon him; otherwise, Allah is most knowing of his capability and will judge him accordingly.[45]

---

44 As long as they do not order that which is disobedience to Allah.

45 Refer also to Ḥadīth No. 34.

Ḥadīth No. 8

عن ابن عمر أن رسول الله (ﷺ) قال:

«أُمِرتُ أَن أُقَاتِلَ النَّاسَ حَتَّى يَشهَدُوا أَن لاَ إِلَهَ إِلاَّ اللهُ وَأَنَّ مُحَمَّدًا رَسُولُ اللهِ، وَيُقِيمُوا الصَّلاَةَ، وَيُؤتُوا الزَّكَاةَ. فَإِذَا فَعَلُوا ذَلِكَ عَصَمُوا مِنِّي دِمَاءَهُم وَأَموَالَهُم، إِلاَّ بِحَقِّ الإِسلاَمِ، وَحِسَابُهُم عَلَى اللهِ تَعَالَى»

On the authority of 'Abdullāh, the son of 'Umar bin al-Khaṭṭāb that the Messenger of Allah (ﷺ) said:

"I have been ordered to fight people until they testify that there is no god but Allah and that Muḥammad is the Messenger of Allah and perform the prayers and give the zakāh. If they do that, they are protected from me regarding their blood and their properties unless by the right of Islam, and their account will be with Allah, the Exalted."

(Narrated by al-Bukhāri and Muslim)

Jihād is one of the most important religious duties in Islam and remains so until the Day of Judgement. It is declared by the head of an Islamic state and supported by the community as a whole. It is not aimed at forcing belief on any people, for the Qur'ān states: لاَ إِكرَاهَ فِي الدِّينِ ***"There shall be no compulsion in religion,"***[46] i.e., in the acceptance of religion. Rather, its purpose is the removal of obstacles to the propagation of Islam and to free thought and choice in the matter, and then the establishment of a force sufficient to uphold this freedom, insure justice and protect Muslims from persecution and oppression.

When the Prophet (ﷺ) was commanded by Allah to fight following the *hijrah* (emigration to al-Madinah) and establishment of the state, Muslims were being persecuted within the Arabian peninsula by the Quraysh and outside its borders by the Persian and Byzantine establishments. Thus, he (ﷺ) was to first liberate the Muslims by subduing opposition among the Arabs, then to continue *jihād* wherever Islam was opposed until men could worship Allah freely and invite others to Islam. The "people" to be fought are those who either attack or persecute Muslims and those who strive to prevent the natural spread of Islam through peaceful means, i.e., through *da`wah* (invitation) and teaching. They may also include apostates, although this category is usually considered separately under "the right of Islam."

It is known that the Messenger of Allah (ﷺ) accepted as a Muslim anyone who pronounced the *shahādah* and regarded his declaration of faith adequate to protect him from being harmed. He required no immediate proof of the person's sincerity and thus strongly rebuked Usāmah bin Zayd for killing a man whom he assumed had said "*Lā illāh ill-Allāh*" only to save himself.

Once a person enters Islam, however, he is expected to fulfill its obligations. A Muslim may be fought by the state for refusing to pray or to give *zakāh* (unlike fasting and *ḥajj*), this having been understood by the *ṣaḥābah* as a part of the "right of Islam." Hence, with the concurrence of other eminent *ṣaḥābah,* Abū Bakr fought the

46 Sūrah al-Baqarah, 2:256.

withholders of *zakāh* after the death of the Prophet (ﷺ) until they finally relented, while some of them, who refused, left the religion altogether. Prayer and *zakāh* are mentioned specifically in the Qur'ān as proof of Islam and protection for those who observe them:

فَإِن تَابُوا وَأَقَامُوا الصَّلَاةَ وَآتَوُا الزَّكَاةَ فَخَلُّوا سَبِيلَهُمْ

> ***"But if they repent, establish prayer and give zakāh, let them go on their way."***[47]

فَإِن تَابُوا وَأَقَامُوا الصَّلَاةَ وَآتَوُا الزَّكَاةَ فَإِخْوَانُكُمْ فِي الدِّينِ

> ***"But if they repent, establish prayer and give zakāh, they are your brothers in religion."***[48]

These verses show that refusal of those two obligations is the reason for continued war against them by the Islamic state.

The "right of Islam" also encompasses the death penalty carried out for capital offenses – those mentioned in the *sunnah,* i.e., murder, adultery and apostasy,[49] or in the Qur'ān, i.e., *ḥirābah,* which includes acts of violence and terrorism against individuals and those of treason and aggression against the Muslim leadership.

Mention of the account with Allah confirms that not every Muslim is sincere in what he professes or does. Hypocrites took care to be seen praying in the mosques in order to insure their safety, and the Prophet (ﷺ) did not permit the killing of anyone who appeared outwardly to be a Muslim in spite of his own knowledge about them. Scholars have agreed that declaration of Islam followed by the outward evidence of prayer and *zakāh* gives one all the rights of a Muslim, including that of protection. If one does that for a worldly benefit, out of fear of death, or dishonestly, such as one who prays without ablution or eats while claiming to be fasting, then Allah is most knowing of him and will judge his deeds accordingly in the Hereafter. But if he is sincere in faith and intention, performing these and other obligations to the best of his ability out of consciousness of Allah, then he is among the ranks of the believers and can expect his full reward.

---

47 Sūrah at-Tawbah, 9:5.

48 Sūrah at-Tawbah, 9:11.

49 See Ḥadīth No. 14.

Hadīth No. 9

عن أبي هريرة عبد الرحمن بن صخر قال: سمعت رسول الله (ﷺ) يقول:
«مَا نَهَيتُكُم عَنهُ فَاجتَنِبُوهُ، وَمَا أَمَرتُكُم بِهِ فَأتُوا مِنهُ مَا استَطَعتُم، فَإِنَّمَا أَهلَكَ الَّذِينَ مِن قَبلِكُم كَثرَةُ مَسَائِلِهِم وَاختِلاَفُهُم عَلَى أَنبِيَائِهِم»

On the authority of Abū Hurayrah, `Abdur-Raḥmān bin Ṣakhr, who said: I heard the Messenger of Allah (ﷺ) say:

"What I have forbidden to you, avoid; what I have ordered you [to do], do of it what you are able. For it was only their excessive questioning and their contradiction of their prophets that destroyed those before you."

(Narrated by al-Bukhāri and Muslim)

Another of the main principles of the religion is defined in these concise words of Allah's Messenger (ﷺ). Upon them are based many *fiqh* rulings concerning different aspects of worship and obedience in general.

First is the avoidance of all which is prohibited (*ḥarām*)[50] without exception. What is normally *ḥarām* but permitted out of dire necessity is not mentioned in this statement since in such a case it is no longer prohibited but has become permissible, at least temporarily. The Prophet (ﷺ) has forbidden to his *ummah* all that is forbidden by Allah, and his order to avoid it is absolute.

In contrast, the order to obey is limited by the extent of one's ability to do so, as Allah has said in the Qur'ān:

لاَ يُكَلِّفُ اللهُ نَفسًا إِلاَّ وُسعَهَا

"Allah does not charge a soul except [with that within] its capacity."[51]

فَاتَّقُوا اللهَ مَا استَطَعتُم

"Fear Allah as much as you are able."[52]

The reason is that there is no inability involved in refraining from something[53] while there could be when intending to perform a duty. Many scholars are of the opinion that because there is no exception to avoidance of the prohibited, it is therefore more important and more virtuous than performing acts of obedience and should take priority. Some have noted also that it is the more difficult of the two because certain temptations might be very strong while the person's natural resistance is weak, requiring him to exert himself forcefully in *jihād* (struggle) against his own soul and to practice the utmost patience and forbearing in avoiding a particular sin; yet, there is no allowance for him in this respect as there is for hardship encountered in carrying out the

50 What is discouraged or disliked (*makrūh*) is not included here, although refraining from it is definitely preferable whenever possible.

51 Sūrah al-Baqarah, 2:286.

52 Sūrah at-Taghābun, 64:16.

53 There could be difficulty, however, such as in cases of addiction. Even so, there is no license to continue in *ḥarām,* and abstinence is enjoined as a positive deed. Avoidance from the outset prevents such conditions from developing.

obligatory duties. For this reason it is noticed that many persons enthusiastically perform pre-dawn prayers and voluntary fasting, while they lack the resolve to desist from such forbidden behavior as cheating, lying, backbiting or disobedience to parents. In reality, repenting and giving up such behavior is no less an act of worship and indeed is an obligatory one which is more pleasing to Allah and averts punishment in the Hereafter. Hence, the saying of some *ṣaḥābah* and their students, "To return a *dirham* taken unlawfully is better than giving a hundred thousand in *ṣadaqah.*" And generally, avoidance of *ḥarām* is an obligation which takes precedence over supplementary worship.

Mention of obedience is followed by the condemnation of its opposite, i.e., procrastination by unnecessary questioning or outright refusal and opposition. An illustration is given in the story of Prophet Mūsā and the Children of Israel when they were commanded by Allah to sacrifice a cow.[54] If they had obeyed their prophet from the very beginning, they would have saved themselves much hardship.

The types of questioning forbidden by the Prophet (ﷺ) on various occasions are

1) personal queries whose answer, if given by the Prophet would have been distressing to the questioner
2) that whose aim is nothing more than argument, ridicule,[55] showing off, or passing time
3) that about purely theoretical situations which have not yet occurred
4) that concerning information which Allah has not revealed

The *ṣaḥābah,* therefore, did not ask questions of this nature and were even severely inhibited from asking about anything in general for fear of sin in that respect. But they admitted that since the Prophet (ﷺ) was usually more lenient with the less informed outsiders, they were pleased when an intelligent man from among the Bedouins inquired about certain aspects of the religion and they could listen to the answers.[56]

Not all questioning is prohibited, however, for there is that which is obligatory, such as the inquiry of an ignorant person about what is required in religion and that which is desirable for obtaining further knowledge. This is especially true after the death of the Prophet (ﷺ), when there is no longer the possibility of further revelation from Allah. Also permissible are questions to those whose knowledge is of benefit in worldly affairs.

What is expected of the student of religion is that he obtain knowledge of what Allah revealed to His Messenger (ﷺ), follow that way, invite to it and teach it. He should seek the rulings given in the Qur'ān and the *sunnah,* exerting every effort to understand them linguistically and historically and then study the pronouncements of the *ṣaḥābah* and *tabi'een* (their followers), giving particular attention to the principles and methods employed by them in *ijtihād.*[57] Although there is disapproval of debates which can lead

54 See Sūrah al-Baqarah, 2:67-71.

55 Referring to the practice of unbelievers.

56 Narrated by Muslim from Anas.

57 The utmost exertion of the mind to reach a correct and appropriate legal ruling. It must be performed by qualified scholars and based upon a thorough analysis of what is relevant of the Qur'ān and sunnah to a particular case or condition.

to animosity and schism, useful discussions based upon a real desire to reach the truth are not only permissible but necessary. The key to this matter is once again a pure intention and fear of Allah while working only for His approval.

Ḥadīth No. 10

عن أبي هريرة قال: قال رسول الله (ﷺ):

«إِنَّ اللهَ تَعَالَى طَيِّبٌ لاَ يَقبَلُ إِلاَّ طَيِّبًا، وَإِنَّ اللهَ أَمَرَ المُؤمِنِينَ بِمَا أَمَرَ بِهِ المُرسَلِينَ، فَقَالَ تَعالَى: يَاأَيُّهَا الرُّسُلُ كُلُوا مِنَ الطَّيِّباتِ وَاعمَلُوا صَالِحًا وَقَالَ تَعالَى يَاأَيُّهَا الَّذِينَ آمَنُوا كُلُوا مِن طَيِّبَاتِ مَا رَزَقنَاكُم ثُمَّ ذَكَرَ الرَّجُلَ يُطِيلُ السَّفَرَ، أَشعَثَ أَغبَرَ، يَمُدُّ يَدَيهِ إِلَى السَّمَاءِ: يَارَبُّ يَارَبُّ، وَمَطعَمُهُ حَرَامٌ، وَمَشرَبُهُ حَرَامٌ وَمَلبَسُهُ حَرَامٌ، وَغُذِيَ بِالحَرَامِ، فَأَنَّى يُستَجَابُ لَهُ»

On the authority of Abū Hurayrah, who reported that the Messenger of Allah (ﷺ) said:

"Indeed, Allah, the Exalted, is pure and accepts only that which is pure. Allah has commanded the believers to do what he commanded the messengers, and He, the Exalted, said: ***'O messengers, eat of the good things and work righteousness.'***[58] And He, the Exalted, said: ***'O you who have believed, eat from the good things with which We have provided you.'***[59] Then he mentioned a man who has prolonged a journey, is disheveled and dusty and extends his hands to the heaven, [supplicating], 'Our Lord, Our Lord,' while his food is unlawful, his drink is unlawful, his clothing is unlawful, and he has been nourished by what is unlawful; so how could he be answered?"

(Narrated by al-Bukhāri and Muslim)

In this ḥadīth the importance of avoiding the unlawful is emphasized from a different perspective: the consequence in the present worldly life as well as in the Hereafter. It teaches that whoever expects his deeds to be accepted by Allah must not pollute them with the unlawful and that the end does not justify the means when it is *ḥarām*. Additionally, a person who would like his supplication to be answered by Allah should take care to consume only what is lawful (*ḥalāl*).

The word "*ṭayyib*" when describing Allah (*subḥānahu wa ta'ālā*), implies the meaning of good and pure or being far removed from any evil or imperfection. When referring to deeds, speech or intention, it means good, pure, sound and lawful. Thus, Allah will not accept a charity from wealth or property gained unlawfully or food that is spoiled. And He will not accept a deed accompanied by pride and showing off or an intention aimed partially at worldly benefit. There is an implication as well that He may not accept the deeds of those who persist in consuming and making use of the unlawful.

---

58 Sūrah al-Mu'minūn, 23:51.

59 Sūrah al-Baqarah, 2:172.

The Muslim *ummah,* being the best nation brought forth as an example to all peoples, has been commanded by Allah to do as the prophets and messengers before them were commanded – namely, to consume the good and lawful foods which Allah has provided, avoiding those that are harmful and therefore prohibited, and to do righteous deeds. This affords evidence that eating good food, when done intending obedience and in order to strengthen the body for carrying out one's obligations (which is itself an obligation), is thus rewarded by Allah. In contrast, one who eats simply out of desire or for enjoyment will not have the same reward as the aforementioned, although he will be rewarded for avoiding *ḥarām* when there is a choice, and Allah knows best.

The Prophet (ﷺ) described the man who has traveled for a long period until he became unkempt and exhausted to illustrate a condition of hardship and humility during which response to supplication is most expected. Commentators have inferred from the context as well that the journey might indeed have been one enjoined by Allah, such as for *ḥajj* or *jihād.* Yet, in spite of that, there remains a preventive factor when such a person calls upon Allah: his unworthiness due to prolonged and continued consumption of *ḥarām.* Reflecting on the final words, "so how could he be answered," one does not conclude that it is entirely impossible, and several verses of the Qur'ān point to the fact that Allah may, for reasons known to Himself, answer the supplication of a disobedient person or a disbeliever and has even granted the request of Iblees, the most evil of creation, saying, ***"Indeed, you are of those reprieved."***[60] The Messenger of Allah (ﷺ) warned, however, that one persisting in the consumption of the unlawful should not expect Allah's aid and that response to his supplication is most unlikely until he repents from that sin.

---

60 See Qur'ān 7:15, 15:37 and 38:80.

Hadīth No. 11

عن أبي محمد الحسن بن على بن أبي طالب سبط رسول الله (ﷺ) وريحانته قال:
حَفِظتُ مِن رَسُولِ اللهِ (ﷺ): «دَع مَا يَرِيبُكَ إِلَى مَا لاَ يَرِيبُكَ»

On the authority of Abū Muḥammad, al-Ḥasan, son of 'Ali bin Abī Ṭālib and grandson of the Messenger of Allah (ﷺ) and his fragrant [i.e., beloved] one, who said:

I memorized from the Messenger of Allah (ﷺ): "Leave that which makes you doubt for that which does not make you doubt."

(Narrated by an-Nasā'i and at-Tirmidhi, who graded it as *ḥasan-ṣaḥeeḥ*)

Included in this ḥadīth are meanings previously cited (in Ḥadīth No. 6) advocating *taqwā* and the avoidance of whatever is doubtful as to its permissibility. Here, there is an additional encouragement to adhere to that about which one is certain, about which the heart feels reassurance rather than anxiety. This principle is one to be applied by the pious person whose deeds are governed by consciousness of Allah at all times. But it is to be pointed out that those who openly and publicly commit unlawful deeds should not involve themselves in questions of this sort nor in the fine points of *fiqh* until they have repented. Ibn 'Umar's disgust at such behavior was evident when he remarked about a delegation from Iraq, "They ask me about the blood of a mosquito while on their hands is the blood of al-Ḥusayn?!"

The principle of basing one's actions upon certainty is also applied to acts of worship. It serves to defeat the attempts of Shayṭān at confusing the worshipper with imaginary fears and distracting him from his worship. Such suggestions (*waswasah*) are to be ignored, and the worshipper must consider as valid that which he knows or remembers for sure.

Thus, when one doubts the number of *rak'ahs* he has prayed, he counts only those of which he is certain and completes his prayer accordingly. The same is true for the number of circuits performed in *ṭawāf*. One may not begin an obligatory act of worship while in doubt whether or not its time has arrived, e.g., not begin prayer until he is sure the *adhān* has been called or its time has passed, and not start the fast of Rama<u>dh</u>ān until he knows the moon has been sighted or that thirty days of Sha'bān have been counted. Certainty must be present at the time of intention.

Or take the case of ablution, where Shayṭān is always prepared to infect the worshipper with suspicion and has delighted in afflicting countless persons with obsessions causing them to waste much water and time, repeatedly interrupt their prayers and even encourage others to do the same. One must understand and believe firmly that water is to be considered pure unless definitely known to be otherwise and that doubt is not sufficient to make it unsuitable for purification. Similarly, doubt is not sufficient to invalidate ablution. When uncertain, one must assume that his ablution is still in effect and continue his worship, making every effort to defeat the strategies of Shayṭān. Obtaining certain knowledge of what does invalidate ablutions will eliminate much of this problem.

Doubt must be dispelled whenever there is an opportunity for obtaining knowledge or finding out the truth. If that is impossible, it should, as a negative influence, be put aside and promptly replaced with a confident adherence to that which is evident and ascertainable.

Hadīth No. 12

عن أبي هريرة قال: قال رسول الله (ﷺ):

«مِن حُسنِ إسلامِ المَرءِ تَركُهُ مَا لاَ يَعنِيهِ»

On the authority of Abū Hurayrah, who said: The Messenger of Allah (ﷺ) said:

"From the excellence of a person's Islam is his leaving alone what does not concern him."

(Narrated by at-Tirmidhi and others in this form – ḥadīth *ḥasan*)

This ḥadīth is considered to be among the fundamental guidelines concerning the perfection of Islam and refining of the soul. While avoiding the prohibited and fulfilling religious obligations makes Islam acceptable, progressing to the degree of *iḥsān*[61] requires that one be always mindful of Allah and of his own manners and behavior, which are means to His pleasure or displeasure. Keeping oneself away from whatever does not concern him is part of the perfecting of his religion and serves to distance him from many doubtful and, indeed, unlawful matters. Hence, one must not intrude uninvited into the affairs of others without necessity and not speak of the affairs of others unnecessarily. This may require no small amount of effort against Shayṭān and against the soul's natural inclination to curiosity.

The directive is most often associated with guarding the tongue, as a similar ḥadīth states: "Indeed, from the excellence of a person's Islam is a sparseness of words about what does not concern him."[62] The Prophet (ﷺ) emphasized the harm in failure to do so when he said to Mu'ādh, "*Does anything topple people onto their faces in the Fire except the fruits of their tongues?*"[63] Ibn Mas'ūd has been quoted as saying, "There is nothing more in need of prolonged imprisonment than my tongue." The *ṣaḥābah* were acutely aware of the dangers of indiscriminate speech. And 'Umar bin 'Abdul-'Azeez observed, "One who counts his speech as part of his deeds will minimize his words except about what concerns him." That is because many people do not consider their statements as accountable deeds, so they are carelessly excessive therein, not usually restricting themselves to truth, discretion and good manners but engaging in gossip or useless debates while raising their voices in accusation or interrupting others with airs of superiority. Such misdeeds will only be eliminated by the silence due to fear of Allah and embarrassment before Him. One should remind others as well, and, when possible,

---

61 See commentary on Ḥadīth No. 2, p. 6.

62 Narrated by Aḥmad and at-Tirmidhi and graded *ḥasan*.

63 See Ḥadīth No. 29.

prevent them from unacceptable speech; otherwise, he should leave the gathering. Allah (*subḥānahu wa ta'ālā*) confirmed the absence of benefit in most discussions, saying:

لاَ خَيرَ فِي كَثِيرٍ مِن نَّجوَاهُم إِلاَّ مَن أَمَرَ بِصَدَقَةٍ أَو مَعرُوفٍ أَو إِصلاَحٍ بَينَ النَّاسِ

"No good is there in much of their private conversation, except for those who enjoin charity or that which is right or conciliation between people."[64]

The Prophet (ﷺ) issued a severe warning when he said, "*Sufficient for a person as sin is his speaking about all that he hears,*"[65] for such speech can hardly be free from untruth or exaggeration or exposure of that which should be concealed. He meant that it is a sin sufficient to place one in Hellfire. Whoever should contemplate the numerous possibilities for sin by the tongue will know that when it is left uncontrolled, one cannot escape commission, so let him instead practice restraint and occupy himself with repentance and the righteous deeds which leave no opportunity for idle pastimes and attention to affairs of no benefit.

64 Sūrah an-Nisaa', 4:114.

65 Narrated by Abū Dāwūd – ṣaḥeeḥ.

Hadīth No. 13

عن أبي حمزة أنس بن مالك خادم رسول الله (ﷺ)، عن النبي (ﷺ) قال:

« لاَ يُؤمِنُ أَحَدُكُم حَتَّى يُحِبَّ لأَخِيهِ مَا يُحِبُّ لِنَفسِهِ»

On the authority of Abū Ḥamzah, Anas bin Mālik, the servant of the Messenger of Allah (ﷺ), that the Prophet (ﷺ) said:

"None of you [truly] believes until he likes for his brother what he likes for himself."

(Narrated by al-Bukhāri and Muslim)

Here, the Prophet (ﷺ) dealt with the subject of faith, which resides in the heart but is reflected in deeds and behavior. Just as perfection of one's Islam entails, among other things, avoiding intrusion into the private affairs of others, perfection of one's *īmān* (belief) necessitates consideration for others and desiring all that is good for them: guidance to Islam, virtuous conduct therein, and it includes the lawful things of this world.

Liking for one's brother what he likes for himself naturally implies disliking for him what he dislikes for himself of evil, harm and difficulty. Such a believer will be apparent by his kind treatment of people, his efforts to help them out in hardships, and his exertion to obtain for them their rights, even if it should cause him some personal difficulty or inconvenience. When one wishes for others what he wishes for himself, he will not compete with them to gain something he already possesses and they lack, nor will he try to deprive them of what he cannot possess himself. He will share his wealth, pass on his knowledge, and give his time for whatever benefits his brothers in this world and the Hereafter. This kind of behavior comes easily from the sound heart of a true believer, while a hypocrite would find it impossible in the absence of a worldly advantage. A heart constrained by bigotry, corrupted with greed or afire with envy cannot contain benevolence at the same time.

An additional concept derived from this ḥadīth is that the true believers are as one single soul, attentive to one another's needs and often preferring their brothers to themselves. One scholar observed, "What is apparent in the ḥadīth is equality [i.e., between the believer and his brother], while in reality it gives preference to the other because everyone likes to be the best and most favored of people; so if he likes the same for his brother, he will have to accept less than that for himself." Opposing the soul's inclination to selfishness is not easy except for those who feel the bond of brotherhood in the cause of Allah.

Although the word "brother" is usually understood to mean a brother in Islam, al-Imām an-Nawawi has suggested a wider concept based upon the common ancestry of mankind. Thus, one should wish for the non-believer what he himself enjoys of faith and contentment within Islam, strive in *da`wah* to him, and supplicate to Allah for his guidance to the truth.

Hadīth No. 14

عن ابن مسعود قال: قال رسول الله (ﷺ):

«لاَ يَحِلُّ دَمُ امرِئٍ مُسلِمٍ إلاَّ بِإحدَى ثَلاَثٍ: الثَّيِّبُ الزَّاني، وَالنَّفسُ بِالنَّفسِ، وَالتَّارِكُ لِدِينِهِ المُفَارِقُ لِلجَمَاعَةِ»

On the authority of Ibn Mas'ūd, who said: The Messenger of Allah (ﷺ) said:

"The blood of a Muslim person is not permitted [to be shed] except in one of three [cases]: the married adulterer, a life for a life,[66] and the renouncer of his religion, the deserter of the community."

(Narrated by al-Bukhāri and Muslim)

The sanctity of a Muslim life is confirmed by the Prophet (ﷺ) in this ḥadīth. The three stated exceptions are those where legal execution is carried out by the state[67] to protect society from the spread of corruption. It may be compared to the surgical removal of a hopelessly diseased limb or organ which, although painful, restores the rest of a body to health. The death penalty, like the lesser prescribed (*ḥadd*) punishments, may only be carried out after a conviction completely free of the least doubt. It must further be established that the accused had reached puberty, was in full mental capacity at the time of the crime, and did not act under any form of coercion.[68] Each of the three will be mentioned briefly:

1) Adultery: After the establishment of moral consciousness in the Muslim community and of legislation that serves as a preventive and after the encouragement and facilitation of lawful marriage, the law deals severely with any who still insist on rebellion which threatens to corrupt both the family and society. The prescribed punishment for married offenders exposes the gravity of this offense, which is greater than in the case of an unmarried fornicator since marriage provides a legal outlet for the sexual instinct as well as security for children of recognized blood relationships within a family.

Besides the verse whose recitation was abrogated while its ruling remained,[69] there are others upon which scholars have based the ruling for adultery. Most often cited are verses 15 and 41-44 of Sūrah al-Mā'idah, which refer to the Prophet's judgement of a case among the Jews according to what Allah had revealed to them in the Torah and upholding the validity of that ruling. Another is in Allah's command:

وَمَا آتَاكُمُ الرَّسُولُ فَخُذُوهُ

"And whatever the Messenger has given you, take."[70]

---

66 i.e., legal retribution for murder.

67 Not independent groups or individuals.

68 See Ḥadīth No. 39.

69 Al-Bukhāri and Muslim have related the speech of 'Umar bin al-Khaṭṭāb in which he said: "Allah sent Muḥammad with the truth and sent down to him the Book. And included in what Allah sent down to him was the verse of stoning. We recited it, memorized it and understood it. The Messenger of Allah (ﷺ) had people stoned to death, and we have done it after him. I fear that if time is prolonged for people, someone may say, 'We do not find stoning in the Book of Allah,' and they would go astray by abandoning an obligation revealed by Allah. And stoning is a true obligation in the Book of Allah, the Exalted, for those who commit adultery when married, of men and women."

70 Sūrah al-Ḥashr, 59:7.

But execution by stoning for the married adulterer is established in the sunnah beyond any doubt. It was carried out by the Prophet (ﷺ) on a few conspicuous occasions but is admittedly a rare occurrance due to the strict conditions that must be fulfilled. First, the offender must be of legal age, sane, free (not a slave), and bound within a marriage where there is no impediment to normal sexual relations. Then it must be proven conclusively that the person committed the crime of his own free will while knowing that it is unlawful. This necessitates either the testimony of four trustworthy male Muslim witnesses that they actually saw the act taking place at a specific time and location (circumstantial evidence is not acceptable) or explicit confession by the guilty party, who should be encouraged at the outset to repent privately to Allah and reform rather than condemn himself to sentence. A confession later retracted prevents the execution, as does the denial of a person named as the partner of a confessing party. Thus, the harshness of this prescribed penalty serves mainly as a practical deterrent and can rarely be carried out.

2) Murder: "A life for a life" means that the life of one who deliberately kills another without right will be taken in turn. Hence, it is not lawful to kill anyone other than the murderer himself, as had been done in the pre-Islamic wars of tribal vengeance. Again, the matter of justice is not left to the victim's family directly but must be referred to the legal authority.

The ruling is clearly stated in the Qur'ān in verses 178 of *Sūrah al-Baqarah* and 45 of *Sūrah al-Mā'idah,* where it is shown that this ordinance was also revealed in the Torah and then upheld in Islam. However, Allah (*subḥānahu wa ta'ālā*) has honored the nation of Prophet Muḥammad (ﷺ) by permitting the acceptance of payment (*diyah*) if the heirs of the victim should choose that option over execution of the murderer.

Some exceptions to the general law of a life for a life have been cited by scholars, although there is no consensus on these matters and differences remain based upon various interpretations of the Qur'ānic verses. It is conceded by all, however, that the sex of both the killer and the victim is irrelevant.

Any case in which a judge rules against execution requires payment to the deceased's heirs of the *diyah.* Besides the possible exceptions or the willingness of the heirs to forego the death penalty, it will not be carried out in case of doubt about the killer's intention, even when he has been convicted of the deed by definite proofs. If willful intent cannot be proved, the *diyah* must be accepted rather than execution, just as in clear cases of accidental killing. Proper legal measures recognized by all serve to put an end to further bloodshed by those who would otherwise seek revenge through acts of violence, perhaps against innocent persons.

3) Apostasy: The meaning portrayed in this ḥadīth is that of *riddah* (reversion) of a sane, mature Muslim from Islam to disbelief of his own free will and his public insistence and propagation of it. It does not include one's private beliefs which have no effect or impact on other members of the community. And it differs from the case of a non-believer who has never entered Islam, because the defiant apostate, through betrayal from within, poses a danger to society. Scholars have also stipulated that the Muslim must once have been conscious of the truth of Islam, not unaware or ignorant. To

completely dispel any doubt, the convicted apostate is allowed a period[71] during which Islam is presented to him anew with the best methods of *da`wah* in the hope that he will return to reason and the religion. He may be executed by the state government only upon adamant and rebellious persistence in *kufr*. Many of the *salaf* (early scholars) interpreted "the renouncer of his religion and deserter of the community" according to the verse of *muḥārabah* (warring),[72] since "waging war against Allah and His Messenger" comprises not only the physical aspect but subversion of the community as well.

A Muslim does not become an apostate by disobedience or sin; rather, only by public denial of divine ordinances or by open claims contrary to the basic tenets of *`aqeedah* (Islamic belief). Some examples are: denial of Allah's oneness; the assertion that some human or other beings have something of divinity within them or have divine attributes; denial of the prophethood of Muḥammad (ﷺ) or claiming there has been a prophet after him; assertions by a person that he has received revelation from Allah; denial of the Hereafter or anything clearly stated in the Qur'ān; ridicule, abuse or denial of any of Allah's prophets, of the Qur'ān or of the sunnah; and declaration of one's preference for humanly devised systems of government or legislation over the divine *Sharī`ah*. A recent convert to Islam would be excused if he made such claims out of ignorance and accepted correction of his views. In addition, anyone forced to save himself by the pronouncement of such statements, his inner faith being unaffected, cannot be regarded as an apostate.

Although the ḥadīth mentions the blood of a Muslim, in this instance it means of the former Muslim who has left Islam. Its wording suggests that among apostates there are those who still claim to be Muslims, utter the *shahādah* and perform some visible duties of Islam. Yet they deceive people and lead them into deviations, thereby weakening the *ummah*. They have deserted the community even when they continue to live within it.

Certain crimes mentioned in the Qur'ān for which the death penalty may be inflicted (namely, "causing corruption in the land" and "waging war against Allah and His Messenger"[73]), generally coincide with the aforementioned, often amounting in reality to willful endangering of life, intentional killing or the form of apostasy evident in treason, conspiracy and drawing arms against innocent Muslims.[74] Jurists have included under these categories a number of crimes perpetrated by threatening death, although the verse of *muḥārabah* also stipulates lesser punishments for those like armed robbery when no one has actually been killed.

And Allah knows best.

---

71 Which is often specified as three days but can be longer.

72 See Sūrah al-Ma'idah, 5:33.

73 See Sūrah al-Ma'idah, 5:32 and 5:33. "Waging war" is explained as committing acts of treason and aggression against the Islamic state or acts of violence and terrorism against unarmed people. Interpreted in the early days of Islam as "highway robbery," other violent crimes are now included. "Corruption," too, has come to encompass a wide range of atrocities, particularly, in recent times, smuggling and dealing in dangerous drugs.

74 Al-Bukhāri and Muslim related from Ibn 'Umar the Prophet's statement: "*Whoever carries arms against us is not from among us.*"

Ḥadīth No. 15

عن أبي هريرة أن رسول الله (ﷺ) قال:

«مَن كَانَ يُؤمِنُ بِاللهِ وَاليَومِ الآخِرِ فَليَقُل خَيرًا أَو لِيَصمُت، وَمَن كَانَ يُؤمِنُ بِاللهِ وَاليَومِ الآخِرِ فَليُكرِم جَارَهُ، وَمَن كَانَ يُؤمِنُ بِاللهِ وَاليَومِ الآخِرِ فَليُكرِم ضَيفَهُ»

On the authority of Abū Hurayrah that the Messenger of Allah (ﷺ) said:

"One who believes in Allah and the Last Day should either speak good or keep silent, and one who believes in Allah and the Last Day should be generous to his neighbor, and one who believes in Allah and the Last Day should be generous to his guest."

(Narrated by al-Bukhāri and Muslim)

"One who believes in Allah and the Last Day" is how the Messenger of Allah (ﷺ) described a sincere servant who has true faith – the kind which saves him from Allah's punishment and obtains for him His approval. Because it shows how to perfect religion through good manners and behavior, the ḥadīth has been called "half of Islam."

The first portion cautions the believer against carelessness in speech, for one who believes in the Last Day must know that his tongue can be a source of harm to him in the Hereafter. In addition to avoiding what does not concern him, as discussed under Ḥadīth No. 12, the believer is commanded here to consider the result of what he wishes to say. If his speech would be deserving of reward from Allah, then it is preferable to silence; otherwise, silence is better for him. Allah has informed us:

مَا يَلفِظُ مِن قَولٍ إِلاَّ لَدَيهِ رَقِيبٌ عَتِيدٌ

"One utters no word except that with him is an observer prepared [to record]."[75]

Some early scholars considered silence a virtue, although this is not an absolute rule. For example, silence in the face of injustice when one is able to prevent it is definitely sinful, as it is when help is needed for someone but no one asks. Good advice and *da'wah* with wisdom should not be neglected. And the Messenger of Allah (ﷺ) warned that failure to mention Allah in a gathering would result in regret on the Day of Judgement. So neither is silence always preferable nor is speech; rather, regard for the outcome of both options in this world and the next is advised. Sufficient in this respect is the ḥadīth narrated by al-Bukhāri: *"Indeed, a servant [of Allah] may say a word that pleases Allah without paying attention to it by which Allah will raise him degrees in rank. And indeed, a servant may say a word that angers Allah without paying attention to it, which will cause him to fall into Hellfire."*

As for neighbors, Allah (*subḥānahu wa ta'ālā*) has ordered good treatment of them in His Book,[76] and the Prophet (ﷺ) recalled that Gabriel continued to counsel him concerning the neighbor until he thought that he might make him an heir.[77]

---

75 Sūrah Qāf, 50:18.

76 See Sūrah an-Nisaa', 4:36.

77 Narrated by al-Bukhāri and Muslim.

The neighbor has been defined as someone who lives in the same house or building, someone who lives next door, someone who lives in the neighborhood (which extends to 40 houses in every direction), and someone who lives in the same town. Upon being asked by his wife, 'Ā'ishah, to which of her two neighbors should she send her gift, the Prophet (ﷺ) replied, "*To the one whose door is nearest you.*"[78]

Generally, one should be concerned about his neighbor and assist him, or at least refrain from annoying him,[79] whether Muslim or non-Muslim, whether near or farther away. At a time when food was considered the best portion of one's wealth, Allah's Messenger (ﷺ) urged sharing it with his neighbors and said, "*The believer is not one who eats his fill while his neighbor is hungry.*"[80]

Generosity to the guest means, first and foremost, pleasant speech and cordial treatment, including service and attention to his needs. Hospitality is normally expressed by offering some kind of food or drink, according to the circumstances of the guest and his host, and generosity is encouraged in this aspect. However, the Prophet (ﷺ) prohibited a guest from causing difficulty for his host[81] and advised the host not to burden himself beyond what is readily available.[82] When someone voluntarily gives preference to a guest over himself or incurs some hardship for his sake, it is out of his own virtue and noble character and not out of Islamic obligation.

Generosity to one's neighbor and guest, when done in obedience and seeking the acceptance of Allah, is an act of worship and therefore should be free of ostentatiousness and extravagance. Accordingly, the reward for this deed will not be diminished if the recipient happens to be wealthy or if what is offered is little in his estimation, and Allah (*subḥānahu wa ta'ālā*) is the best judge of intentions.

---

78 Narrated by al-Bukhāri.

79 This is the minimum of one's duty toward his neighbor.

80 Narrated by al-Hakim and aṭ-Ṭabarāni – *ṣaḥeeḥ*.

81 In a ḥadīth narrated by al-Bukhāri and Muslim.

82 In a ḥadīth graded *ṣaḥeeḥ* narrated by Aḥmad and aṭ-Ṭabarāni.

Hadīth No. 16

عن أبي هريرة:

أَنَّ رَجُلاً قَالَ لِلنَّبِيِّ (ﷺ): أَوصِنِي، قَالَ: «لاَ تَغضَب»، فَرَدَّدَ مِرَارًا، قَالَ: «لاَ تَغضَب»

On the authority of Abū Hurayrah, who said:

A man said to the Prophet (ﷺ): "Counsel me." He (ﷺ) said, "Do not get angry." The man repeated [his request] several times. He (ﷺ) said, "Do not get angry."

(Narrated by al-Bukhāri)

In his commentary al-Imām an-Nawawi pointed out that what is meant here is that a Muslim should not act upon his anger, since anger itself is a natural human reaction to being faced with what one dislikes. And although a person cannot prevent its occurrence, especially when his sense of justice has been outraged, he can train himself to react in a wise manner that is pleasing to Allah. Thus, the first concern is control until one is able to think rationally.

In a ḥadīth similar to this one[83] the man concluded, "So I thought about what the Prophet (ﷺ) had said and realized that anger comprises all evil." The Prophet's observation that "*Anger is from Shayṭān, and Shayṭān was created from fire*"[84] suggests that Shayṭān continually strives to anger people and justify their anger to them so that they will lose their balance, speak sinfully, commit crimes, and preserve hatred and resentment in their hearts, causing them to behave in ways that will insure his companionship in the fire of Hell.

Therefore, the Messenger of Allah (ﷺ) prescribed certain methods for lessening anger or at least enabling a believer to avoid the trap of Shayṭān and resist a reaction he could later regret. Among them is the performance of ablution (*wudhu'*), according to the aforementioned narration, which continues: "*Shayṭān was created from fire, but fire can be put out with water; so when one of you becomes angry, let him perform wudhu'.*" Another remedy mentioned by Allah's Messenger (ﷺ) is related by al-Bukhāri. Upon seeing a man enraged at another, he (ﷺ) said, "*I know a word that, if he said it, would remove what affects him: A`ūdhu billāhi min ash-Shayṭānir-rajeem.*"[85]

On another occasion he (ﷺ) said, "*When one of you becomes angry while standing, let him be seated; and if his anger does not depart, let him lie down.*"[86] Scholars commented that one who is standing is in a position to take revenge, while one sitting is less prepared for that, and one stretched out on the ground is in the state of least readiness. Thus, the Prophet (ﷺ) intended to distance the angry person from confrontation until his anger had subsided. He (ﷺ) also corrected the assumption that such behavior could be seen as weakness when he said, "*The strong one is not he who throws someone down; the strong one is only he who controls himself when angry.*"[87]

83 Narrated by Aḥmad and Ibn Ḥibbān, who graded it ṣaḥeeḥ.

84 Narrated by Aḥmad and Abū Dāwūd – ḥasan.

85 "I seek refuge in Allah from Shayṭān, the expelled," i.e., the evicted or driven away from Allah's mercy.

86 Narrated by Aḥmad and Abū Dāwūd – ṣaḥeeḥ.

87 Narrated by al-Bukhāri and Muslim.

His own example was reported by many of his companions. If he (ﷺ) disliked something, it would show in his face, but he spoke only when the matter concerned something that would anger Allah. He never struck a servant or a woman and never took revenge for personal grievances, only fighting for the cause of Allah. Among his supplications was, "O Allah, I ask you for the word of truth in anger and in pleasure,"[88] and his manner, as reported by 'Ā'ishah, was that of the Qur'ān,[89] wherein Allah praised ***"those who restrain anger and pardon the people"***[90] and those ***"who, when they are angry, forgive."***[91]

If one has not attained the ability to overlook his brother's transgression or if it involves the rights of others, he may seek justice through the legal authority. But one who strikes out with his hand or tongue in a fit of anger rarely stops at the limit of what is due to him, thereby becoming an aggressor himself and giving the advantage to his opponent in the account of the Hereafter. He will be held responsible by law in this world, as well, for any damage he might cause to person or property during failure to control his rage.

This ḥadīth deals with anger that results from personal affront and obviously does not include that caused by the violation of Allah's rights or those of His creatures, which should incite the Muslim to defend and demand justice according to his ability; for this is praiseworthy and an aspect of virtue.

---

88 A portion of a ḥadīth narrated by Aḥmad and an-Nasā'i and graded ṣaḥeeḥ.

89 Narrated by Aḥmad and Muslim.

90 Sūrah Ali 'Imran, 3:134.

91 Sūrah ash-Shūrā, 42:37.

Ḥadīth No. 17

عن أبي يعلى شداد بن أوس عن رسول الله (ﷺ) قال:

« إِنَّ اللهَ كَتَبَ الإِحسَانَ عَلَى كُلِّ شَيءٍ، فَإِذَا قَتَلتُم فَأَحسِنُوا القِتلَةَ، وَإِذَا ذَبَحتُم فَأَحسِنُوا الذِّبحَةَ،
وَليُحِدَّ أَحَدُكُم شَفرَتَهُ، وَليُرِح ذَبِيحَتَهُ»

On the authority of Abū Ya'la, Shaddād bin Aus, that the Messenger of Allah (ﷺ) said:

"Indeed, Allah has decreed *iḥsān* for all things. So when you kill, kill well; and when you slaughter, slaughter well. Let each one of you sharpen his blade, and let him spare suffering to the animal he slaughters."

(Narrated by Muslim)

The concept of *iḥsān* was discussed briefly under Ḥadīth No. 2. Its general meaning is "doing something well" or "as well as possible." Several rulings are inferred from the opening statement: first, that Allah (*subḥānahu wa ta'ālā*) has made *iḥsān* a duty incumbent upon all creation; second, that He has made it a duty toward all things and all creatures; and third, that He has made *iḥsān* an obligation in all things, i.e., in every job or deed one performs. Thus, it has been described as good treatment, good conduct, perfection of religion, etc.

Good treatment is ordained by Allah toward any person or animal that is to be killed lawfully, which means making the death as swift and easy as possible, sparing any unnecessary pain and anguish. After the mention of killing in general, the Prophet (ﷺ) specifically ordered *iḥsān* in the slaughter of animals for food.

The Messenger of Allah (ﷺ) gave various details concerning the proper way to slaughter in several narrations, which al-Imām Aḥmad and others have summarized as follows:

The animal should be led gently to the place of slaughter, without frightening it or pulling it roughly. It should be offered water to drink if thirsty. The knife should be well sharpened to cause the least amount of pain, and it should be concealed from the animal before the moment of use.[92] In addition, the slaughter should not take place in the presence of other animals, for even a dumb animal is aware of two things: its Lord and death, which it fears. Finally, it should be turned toward the *qiblah* if possible and the name of Allah mentioned over it at the time of slaughter. The throat should be cut with one stroke and deeply through the jugular veins so that death will come quickly. Then the animal should be left to toss about freely while the blood drains and should not be cut again before it is dead. It is reported that a man said to Allah's Messenger (ﷺ), "When I slaughter a sheep, I am merciful to her." He (ﷺ) replied, "*If you are merciful to the sheep, Allah will be merciful to you.*"[93]

---

92 In a ḥadīth related by aṭ-Ṭabarāni and rated as ṣaḥeeḥ, it is reported that once the Prophet (ﷺ) came across a man holding a sheep to the ground with his foot and sharpening his blade while the sheep looked at him. He (ﷺ) addressed him, saying, "*Couldn't you have done it [i.e., the sharpening] before this? Do you want to cause her numerous deaths?!*"

93 From *Musnad Aḥmad* – ṣaḥeeḥ.

Hadīth No. 18

عن أبي ذر جندب بن جنادة وأبي عبد الرحمن معاذ بن جبل عن رسول الله (ﷺ) قال:

«اتَّقِ اللهَ حَيثُمَا كُنتَ، وَأَتبِعِ السَّيِّئَةَ الحَسَنَةَ تَمحُهَا، وَخَالِقِ النَّاسَ بِخُلُقٍ حَسَنٍ»

On the authority of Abū Dharr, Jundub bin Junādah, and Abū `Abdur-Raḥmān, Mu'ādh bin Jabal, that the Messenger of Allah (ﷺ) said:

"Fear Allah wherever you are and follow up a bad deed with a good one; it will wipe it out, and deal with people by good moral character."

(Narrated by at-Tirmidhi – *ḥasan-ṣaḥeeḥ*)

This ḥadīth contains comprehensive instruction concerning the rights of Allah and rights of people. The first of these is an admonition to fear Allah at every time and place, whether among others or alone; more specifically, to fear the displeasure and anger of Allah and to fear His punishment. The general meanings embodied in the verb "*ittaqa*" are protection and prevention, caution and avoidance; thus, the believer is advised to prevent and protect himself from the consequence of unlawful deeds by avoiding them altogether. It is accomplished by obeying Allah conscientiously and constantly, remembering that He sees everything one does and is aware of his innermost secrets. *Taqwā*[94] in itself is commanded repeatedly by Allah in the Qur'ān and is therefore a primary obligation upon every Muslim.

The righteous caliph, `Umar bin `Abdul-'Azeez, said, "*Taqwā* is not fasting by day, praying by night and other such things, but *taqwā* is refraining from what Allah has prohibited and doing what Allah has commanded. And whoever has been provided with good[95] beyond that – it is additional good." And he wrote to someone, saying, "I recommend to you the fear [*taqwā*] of Allah, the Mighty and Majestic, who accepts only that, has mercy upon its people, and rewards for it; for those who advise it are many, and those who practice it are few. May Allah make us and you among those who have *taqwā*."

Since every servant of Allah is ordered to have *taqwā* both openly and privately in spite of the fact that he is bound to commit sins, the Prophet (ﷺ) directed the believer how to eliminate his misdeeds by following them with good ones,[96] primarily, repentance as soon as one realizes his error and apology to Allah.[97] Hence, taking account of the self continuously is also prescribed so that one may rectify his condition before it is permanently inscribed in his record.

It is possible that in this ḥadīth the Prophet (ﷺ) was referring to other good deeds beyond repentance or to the acts of worship, such as performance of ablution and prayer, praising Allah, going for *ḥajj* and *'umrah,* fasting, etc., which serve as a *kaffārah* (expiation for sins). He (ﷺ) stipulated in several other narrations, however, that such

---

94 Consciousness and fear of Allah.

95 i.e., opportunities for extra worship.

96 This is in accordance with what Allah (*subḥānahu wa ta`ālā*) has stated in Sūrah Hūd, 11:114.

97 Al-Imām an-Nawawi pointed out that although repentance is sufficient to repair the relationship between the servant and Allah once it is accepted, if the offense concerns the right of another human being, reparation must be made or the offender forgiven by the one he harmed.

deeds remove the errors and lesser sins for those who avoid all the major sins. A major sin can be annulled only by immediate, complete and sincere repentance, which is in itself ordained by Allah for every believer.[98] This consists of intense regret and the realization that one has angered his Lord, immediate cessation of the transgression, and earnestly seeking the forgiveness of Allah through prayer, supplication and the performance of additional good deeds. Allah (*subḥānahu wa ta'ālā*) has confirmed:

وَإِنِّي لَغَفَّارٌ لِمَن تَابَ وَآمَنَ وَعَمِلَ صَالِحًا ثُمَّ اهْتَدَى

> ***"Indeed, I am the Perpetual Forgiver of whoever repents and believes and does righteousness and then remains rightly guided."***[99]

Behaving well toward people is in reality one aspect of *taqwā*; indeed, without it *taqwā* is deficient. Allah (*subḥānahu wa ta'ālā*) has described people with *taqwā* as:

الَّذِينَ يُنفِقُونَ فِي السَّرَّاءِ وَالضَّرَّاءِ وَالْكَاظِمِينَ الْغَيْظَ وَالْعَافِينَ عَنِ النَّاسِ

> ***"...Those who spend [on others] during ease and hardship and restrain anger and pardon the people."***[100]

The Prophet (ﷺ) mentioned good behavior separately in this ḥadīth because there is a need to emphasize this particular aspect of *taqwā,* for many people are of the opinion that righteousness means attention to Allah's rights alone. Thus, they devote themselves to worship while often neglecting the rights of their fellow men. Therefore, on numerous occasions the Messenger (ﷺ) stressed the importance of good character, saying, "*The best of the believers is the best of them in character,*"[101] and "*Indeed, the believer, through good character, reaches the ranks of one who fasts [by day] and prays [by night].*"[102]

---

98 As in Sūrah an-Nūr, 24:31, Sūrah al-Ḥujurāt, 49:11, and Sūrah at-Taḥreem, 66:8, among others.

99 Sūrah Ṭā Hā, 20:82.

100 Sūrah Aali 'Imrān, 3:134.

101 Ibn Mājah and al-Ḥākim – ṣaḥeeḥ. These and similar words are contained in quite a number of ṣaḥeeḥ and ḥasan narrations.

102 Narrated by Abū Dāwūd – ṣaḥeeḥ.

Hadīth No. 19

عن أبي العباس عبد الله بن العباس قال:

كُنْتُ خَلْفَ النَّبِيِّ (ﷺ) يَوْمًا فَقَالَ لِي «يَا غُلَامُ، إِنِّي أُعَلِّمُكَ كَلِمَاتٍ: احْفَظِ اللهَ يَحْفَظْكَ، احْفَظِ اللهَ تَجِدْهُ تُجَاهَكَ، إِذَا سَأَلْتَ فَاسْأَلِ اللهَ، وَإِذَا اسْتَعَنْتَ فَاسْتَعِنْ بِاللهِ، وَاعْلَمْ أَنَّ الْأُمَّةَ لَوِ اجْتَمَعَتْ عَلَى أَنْ يَنْفَعُوكَ بِشَيْءٍ لَمْ يَنْفَعُوكَ إِلَّا بِشَيْءٍ قَدْ كَتَبَهُ اللهُ لَكَ، وَإِنِ اجْتَمَعُوا عَلَى أَنْ يَضُرُّوكَ بِشَيْءٍ لَمْ يَضُرُّوكَ إِلَّا بِشَيْءٍ قَدْ كَتَبَهُ اللهُ عَلَيْكَ رُفِعَتِ الْأَقْلَامُ وَجَفَّتِ الصُّحُفُ».

(رواه الترمذي وقال: حديث حسن صحيح)

وفي رواية غير الترمذي:

«احْفَظِ اللهَ تَجِدْهُ أَمَامَكَ، تَعَرَّفْ إِلَى اللهِ فِي الرَّخَاءِ يَعْرِفْكَ فِي الشِّدَّةِ، وَاعْلَمْ أَنَّ مَا أَخْطَأَكَ لَمْ يَكُنْ لِيُصِيبَكَ، وَمَا أَصَابَكَ لَمْ يَكُنْ لِيُخْطِئَكَ، وَاعْلَمْ أَنَّ النَّصْرَ مَعَ الصَّبْرِ، وَأَنَّ الْفَرَجَ مَعَ الْكَرْبِ، وَأَنَّ مَعَ الْعُسْرِ يُسْرًا».

On the authority of Abū ʿAbbās, ʿAbdullāh bin ʿAbbās, who said:

One day I was [mounted] behind the Prophet (ﷺ), and he said to me, "Young man, I will teach you words [of advice]: Keep Allah in mind – He will keep you from harm. Keep Allah in mind – you will find Him before you. When you ask, ask Allah; and when you seek help, seek it from Allah. Know that even if the [whole] nation assembled in order to benefit you with something, it could not benefit you except by something Allah had already decreed for you; and if they assembled in order to harm you with something, they could not harm you except with something Allah had already decreed upon you. The pens have been lifted, and the pages have dried."

(Narrated by at-Tirmidhi – ḥasan-ṣaḥeeḥ)

And in a narration by other than at-Tirmidhi:

"Keep Allah in mind – you will find Him in front of you. Come to know Allah in times of ease – He will know you in times of hardship. And know that whatever missed you could not have struck you, and whatever struck you could not have missed you. And know that help comes with patience and that relief accompanies distress and that with hardship will come ease."

Here are found some of the most important precepts of the religion. Ibn al-Jawzi said, "I contemplated this ḥadīth and it amazed me; I almost lost my head. How regrettable is ignorance of this ḥadīth and deficiency in understanding its meanings." Of the many details and examples cited by various scholars, a general outline may be derived:

The word "*ḥifth*"[103] embodies the meanings of keeping, retaining, preserving, protecting, guarding and maintaining. Thus, "keeping Allah in mind" is not limited to remembering Him but includes obeying His commands and maintaining His rights and limits, as if one was guarding a sacred territory. The result of such care is that Allah (*subḥānahu wa taʿālā*) will protect and keep his servant from harm.

---

103 Which is the source of "*iḥfath*," the verb used in the text of the ḥadīth.

Allah's protection is of two kinds: that of his physical self, family and property by means of angels, and what is better – protection of the servant's faith and religion. For he who keeps the commands of Allah will be kept on the straight path, protected from going astray or committing major sins and kept firm at the time of death. Ibn 'Abbās alluded to these meanings in his *tafseer* (explanation) of the Qur'ān's words:

وَاعلَمُوا أَنَّ اللهَ يَحُولُ بَينَ المَرءِ وَقَلبِهِ

"And know that Allah intervenes between a man and his heart."[104]

When one keeps Allah in mind in the ways previously stated, a second result (specified in both ḥadīths) is that he will find Allah before him, i.e., with him through every difficulty, guiding him and reassuring his heart. Additional clarification is given in the second ḥadīth, for when one establishes a good relationship with his Lord through obedience and *taqwā* in times of ease and prosperity, he can expect aid from Him during hardship and affliction.[105] Among the most difficult times one faces is that of death. Therefore, he should prepare adequately for it beforehand by turning to the only one who can ease his soul's departure from the world and save him from the torments of Hell.

The next instruction, to ask and seek help from Allah, encourages reliance upon Him alone as the sole deity and source of benefit and harm. There is an implication that all human beings are in need of assistance throughout their lives and that they will ask it of whomever or whatever they deem capable. The believer will turn in supplication to his Lord, knowing that any aid from his fellow men and any means he employs to an end will only succeed if Allah wills it and that He (*subḥānahu wa ta'ālā*) is able and competent to accomplish whatever He wills, even when it appears insurmountable to man. Allah has said:

ادعُونِي أَستَجِب لَكُم

"Call upon Me; I will respond to you."[106]

At the same time, Allah (*subḥānahu wa ta'ālā*) has predestined every occurrence, so the Prophet (ﷺ) reminded us that nothing could have changed what was destined to occur. This gives comfort and encourages patience at times of distress. In the words of the Qur'ān:

مَا أَصَابَ مِن مُصِيبَةٍ فِي الأَرضِ وَلاَ فِي أَنفُسِكُم إِلاَّ فِي كِتَابٍ مِن قَبلِ أَن نَبرَأَهَا إِنَّ ذَلِكَ عَلَى اللهِ يَسِيرٌ لِكَيلاَ تَأسَوا عَلَى مَا فَاتَكُم وَلاَ تَفرَحُوا بِمَا آتَاكُم

"No disaster strikes upon the earth or among yourselves except that it is in a register before We bring it into being. Indeed, that, for Allah, is easy. [It is] in order that you not despair over what has eluded you and not exult over what He has given you..."[107]

---

104 Sūrah al-Anfāl, 8:24.

105 As a means of trial, Allah (*subḥānahu wa ta'ālā*) may respond to the supplication of a disobedient servant or even a disbeliever in a desperate situation. Such a person fails the test when thereafter he returns to heedlessness instead of repenting to his Lord.

106 Sūrah Ghāfir, 40:60.

107 Sūrah al-Ḥadeed, 57:22-23.

Many adverse conditions may be changed through physical efforts or due to a person's supplication, but this has also been decreed by Allah. And we should know that every occurrence is the result of a cause, by His decree, and that man was given a limited ability, by His decree, for which he is held responsible.[108]

Since the servant is often unaware of how he is being protected by Allah or of what good Allah has in store for him, he must put his trust in Him and accept whatever has been decreed for him. Gracious acceptance is superior to patience in that it reflects true submission and trust. Among the Prophet's supplications was, "*O Allah, I ask of You acceptance [by me] after the decree.*"[109] And he (ﷺ) said, "*When Allah loves a people, he gives them trials. So whoever accepts will be accepted [by Allah], and whoever becomes angry will obtain anger.*"[110]

The lifting or removal of pens and drying of ink on the pages is an allegorical reference to something which has long since been completed and finalized and is in no way subject to alteration. And the conclusion of the second ḥadīth gives hope and repels despair, reminding again that although all men – and especially the righteous among them – are continuously exposed to trials and afflictions of every kind, the believer, by trusting in Allah, supplicating Him fervently, practicing patience, and accepting His decree, can be sure that relief will come as Allah (*subḥānahu wa ta'ālā*) has promised.[111]

---

108 See explanation under Ḥadīth No. 4.

109 Part of a ḥadīth narrated by an-Nasā'i and al-Ḥākim – ṣaḥeeḥ.

110 Narrated by at-Tirmidhi – *ḥasan.*

111 In the Qur'ān – Sūrah at-Ṭalāq, 65:7 and Sūrah ash-Sharḥ, 94:5-6.

Ḥadīth No. 20

عن أبي مسعود عقبة بن عمرو الأنصاري البدري قال: قال رسول الله (ﷺ):

«إِنَّ مِمَّا أَدرَكَ النَّاسُ مِن كَلَامِ النُّبُوَّةِ الأُولَى: إِذَا لَم تَستَحِ فَاصنَع مَا شِئتَ»

On the authority of Abū Mas'ūd, 'Uqbah bin 'Amr al-Anṣāri al-Badri, who said: The Messenger of Allah (ﷺ) said:

"Among that which people knew from the words of former prophecy is: When you feel no shame, then do whatever you wish."

(Narrated by al-Bukhāri)

The Messenger of Allah (ﷺ) has confirmed the excellence of an ancient virtue which affects one's behavior both in public and private matters. We understand from him that these very words were spoken by earlier prophets and that people memorized them and passed them down from generation to generation.

"*Al-ḥayā'*"[112] can best be described as shyness and sensitivity toward another. It may be accompanied by a feeling of embarrassment or shame over the other's knowledge of one's shortcomings. It has been noted that modesty and shyness can be a part of the inborn moral character, or it can be acquired through knowledge of Allah, and this, especially, is what the Prophet (ﷺ) praised as being a part of the faith.[113] Shyness from Allah, the all-Aware, prevents the servant from deeds and thoughts that might appear ugly in His sight and prompts immediate repentance whenever he should slip. As a recipient of Allah's countless favors, he is ashamed to offend his benefactor from whom nothing is concealed and who said:

أَلَم يَعلَم بِأَنَّ اللهَ يَرَى

"Does he not know that Allah sees?"[114]

The words quoted in this ḥadīth have been interpreted thus:

1) As a statement of fact – i.e., a person who feels no shame will disregard everyone including his Lord and will do whatever he pleases.
2) As a permission – i.e., if that which a person considers doing will not cause him embarrassment before other Muslims and particularly before his Lord, then he may proceed.
3) As a threat – i.e., if you feel no shame over your evil deeds and intentions, then do whatever you will, for Allah will take you to account for it and punish you accordingly.

إِنَّ اللهَ كَانَ عَلَيكُم رَقِيبًا

"Indeed Allah is ever, over you, an Observer."[115]

---

112 From which is derived the verb form used in this narration.
113 In narrations by al-Bukhāri and Muslim.
114 Sūrah al-'Alaq, 96:14.
115 Sūrah an-Nisaa', 4:1.

Ḥadīth No. 21

عن أبي عمرو – وقيل أبي عمرة – سفيان بن عبد الله قال:

قُلْتُ: يَا رَسُولَ اللهِ، قُلْ لِي فِي الإِسْلاَمِ قَوْلاً لاَ أَسْأَلُ عَنْهُ أَحَدًا غَيْرَكَ، قَالَ: «قُلْ: آمَنْتُ بِاللهِ، ثُمَّ اسْتَقِمْ»

On the authority of Abū 'Amr – and he is also mentioned as Abū 'Amrah – Sufyān bin 'Abdullāh, who said:

I said, "O Messenger of Allah, tell me something about Islam which I will not [need to] ask anyone but you." He said, "Say, 'I believe in Allah,' and then remain upright."

(Narrated by Muslim)

The request of this companion was a very particular one. It was for advice that would enable him to live successfully within Islam, but advice so clear that he would not need anyone to explain further and so complete that he would not need anyone to add to it thereafter. The reply of the Prophet (ﷺ) was concise yet comprehensive, including all the meanings of *īmān* (faith) and Islam, for he ordered him to reaffirm the faith in his heart and then prove his faith by remaining upright according to its requirements.

Being upright means adhering continuously to the straight path laid out by Allah (*subḥānahu wa ta'ālā*), which is free from crookedness and deviation. The basis of uprightness, according to Abū Bakr aṣ-Ṣiddeeq, is *tawḥeed* and sincerity to Allah. It has further been defined as complete obedience to Allah and sincerity to Him in faith and deeds (which is the essence of *tawḥeed*), i.e., behaving toward Allah with the knowledge that He alone is one's Lord.

It has been noted that many people have said, "Our Lord is Allah" and then proved otherwise. Evidence of one's faith is in his behavior, therefore 'Umar bin al-Khaṭṭāb described "remaining upright" as upright to Allah in obedience to Him, not evading like the swerving of a fox.

A true and certain knowledge that one's Lord is Allah comes from the knowledge of His perfect and absolute attributes. This establishes in the heart the awe, fear, love and hope which makes the body subservient in upright conduct. Allah (*subḥānahu wa ta'ālā*) ordained that we ask His guidance in remaining on the right course in every *rak'ah* of prayer, saying:

اهدِنَا الصِّرَاطَ المُستَقِيمَ

"Guide us to the straight path,"[116]

i.e., keep us there and return us to it whenever we err and deviate. And He informed us:

إِنَّ الَّذِينَ قَالُوا رَبُّنَا اللهُ ثُمَّ اسْتَقَامُوا تَتَنَزَّلُ عَلَيْهِمُ المَلَائِكَةُ أَلَّا تَخَافُوا وَلَا تَحْزَنُوا وَأَبْشِرُوا بِالجَنَّةِ الَّتِي كُنتُمْ تُوعَدُونَ

"Indeed, those who have said, 'Our Lord is Allah' and then remained upright – the angels will descend upon them, [saying], 'Do not fear

---

[116] Sūrah al-Fātiḥah, 1:6.

and do not grieve, but receive good tidings of Paradise which you were promised.' "[117]

Thus, the outcome of being upright within Islam is no less than security on the Day of Resurrection and Paradise as promised by Allah (*subḥānahu wa ta`ālā*). Every Muslim should aspire for this as did al-Ḥasan bin 'Ali, who supplicated, "O Allah, You are our Lord, so endow us with uprightness."

Ḥadīth No. 22

عن أبي عبد الله جابر بن عبد الله الأنصاري:

أَنَّ رَجُلاً سَأَلَ رَسُولَ اللهِ (ﷺ) فَقَالَ: أَرَأَيتَ إِذَا صَلَّيتُ المَكتُوبَاتِ، وَصَمتُ رَمَضَانَ، وَأَحلَلتُ الحَلاَلَ، وَحَرَّمتُ الحَرَامَ، وَلَم أَزِد عَلَى ذَلِكَ شَيئًا، أَدخُلُ الجَنَّةَ؟ قَالَ «نَعَم»

On the authority of Abū `Abdullāh, Jābir bin `Abdullāh al-Anṣāri:

A man asked the Messenger of Allah (ﷺ), "Do you consider: if I prayed the obligatory prayers, fasted Ramadhān, allowed what is lawful and prohibited what is unlawful and added nothing to that, I would enter Paradise?" He said, "Yes."

(Narrated by Muslim)

Some of the commentators on this ḥadīth have mentioned that the man who approached the Prophet (ﷺ) with this question was one who had recently accepted Islam. In light of this fact, certain conclusions may be drawn:

1) The Prophet (ﷺ) wanted to clarify the difference between what is obligatory in the religion and additional voluntary deeds, for which there is no blame if one does not perform them.

2) Since the man seemed unwilling at that point to take on more than he mentioned, the Prophet (ﷺ) did not want to discourage him by adding anything further. He knew, as he had said to some of his companions on similar occasions, that once true faith had entered his heart, this man would himself seek to increase his deeds. With some individuals, particularly new converts and young Muslims, one should not press beyond the obligatory duties for fear of overburdening them at a stage when they are not yet prepared to do more than that. And how many youths, having fallen short of the demands of pious elders, gave up altogether for some years. For this reason the Messenger of Allah (ﷺ) has said, "*Facilitate and do not make difficulty; give good tidings and do not cause aversion.*"[118] Thus, the ḥadīth possibly reflects an allowance due to a temporary circumstance.

3) All of what will be judged by Allah of intentions and attitudes of the heart and actions and expressions of the body is either lawful or unlawful. Hence, if the man kept himself from everything *ḥarām,* which includes the neglect of all obligatory

117 Sūrah Fuṣṣilat, 41:30. Similar words are repeated in Sūrah al-Aḥqāf, 46:13-14.

118 Narrated by al-Bukhāri and Muslim.

duties beyond the ones he mentioned, he would thereby enter Paradise. Therefore, the ḥadīth can also be seen as general and comprehensive.

Although the Prophet (ﷺ) accepted as sufficient the deeds mentioned by this man, it is known that his companions and all righteous Muslims after them, following his example and instruction, did not limit themselves to obligations but exerted the utmost efforts in every kind of additional worship, seeking acceptance from Allah and knowing that their deeds could never be adequate. In fact, the scholars have always agreed that to deliberately avoid the Prophet's sunnah is in itself sinful. Supererogatory worship is encouraged to make up for deficiencies in the obligatory, and imperfection is a human attribute. Therefore, to neglect the sunnah would amount to a deficiency in one's religion, but Allah knows best.

Ḥadīth No. 23

عن أبي مالك الحارث بن عاصم الأشعري قال: قال رسول الله (ﷺ):

«الطُّهُورُ شَطرُ الإِيمَانِ، وَالحَمدُ لِلهِ تَملأ المِيزَانَ، وَسُبحَانَ اللهِ وَالحَمدُ لِلهِ تَملآنِ – أَو تَملأ – مَا بَينَ السَّمَاءِ وَالأَرضِ، وَالصَّلاَةُ نُورٌ، وَالصَّدَقَةُ بُرهَانٌ، وَالصَّبرُ ضِيَاءٌ، وَالقُرآنُ حُجَّةٌ لَكَ أَو عَلَيكَ. كُلُّ النَّاسِ يَغدُو فَبَائِعٌ نَفسَهُ فَمُعتِقُهَا أَو مُوبِقُهَا»

On the authority of Abū Mālik, al-Ḥārith bin 'Aasim al-Ash'ari, who said: The Messenger of Allah (ﷺ) said:

"Purity is half the faith. And *'al-ḥamdu lillāh'*[119] fills the scale; and *'subḥān Allāh'*[120] and *'al-ḥamdu lilāah'* fill what is between the heaven and earth. Prayer is light, *ṣadaqah* is evidence, patience is burning light, and the Qur'ān is an argument for you or against you. Each of the people begins at morning, selling his soul – either freeing it [thereby] or destroying it."

(Narrated by Muslim)

The majority of commentators have considered that "purity" in this narration refers to bodily purification or ablution. Al-Imām an-Nawawi, however, preferred the interpretation "purity of the heart" from such ailments as envy, hatred, conceit, etc., adding that faith cannot be complete without it. It is possible that the general term "purity" includes both kinds – physical and spiritual. The phrase "half the faith" is used in the sense of a portion rather than the specification of exactly one half; in short, a significant part of the faith.

The texts of the Qur'ān and ḥadīth state that good deeds have weight and that one whose balance of deeds is heavy at the time of Judgement will have earned a great reward. Praising Allah with the tongue, and more importantly, in the heart under every condition, earns as much reward as the good deeds which fill the balance. The addition

119 "Praise be to Allah" or "all praise [is due] to Allah."

120 "Far removed is Allah above every imperfection," i.e., exalted is He above that.

to it of "*subḥān Allāh*" earns additional reward, the capacity of what is between the heaven and earth. Thus, scholars have inferred that the praise of Allah for His perfection (*al-hamdu lillāh*) is greater than the disassociation of Him from all imperfection (*subḥān Allāh*), since the capacity of the balance is greater than that of the heaven and earth and whatever lies between them.

Prayer is described as "*nūr,*" i.e., pure light in a general, unspecified sense. It is light for the believers throughout their worldly life, enlightening their hearts and minds and showing the straight path which leads to Allah. It is comparable to the glow of moonlight (which the Qur'ān also describes as *nūr*) and is often evident in their faces. It is also light for them in the Hereafter, within the darknesses of the Day of Resurrection and on the path which leads them over the Hellfire to Paradise.

Ṣadaqah, which includes both the obligatory *zakāh* and voluntary charities, is clear evidence of faith on the Day of Judgement because it will not be found with the hypocrite. "*Burhān*" is a form of light as well (a sunbeam) which illuminates and shows the existence of something, i.e., an evidence or proof.

Patience is "*ḏḥiyā',*" a burning light (a name the Qur'ān gives to the sun), possibly because of the great effort that goes into it. Patience in the face of what one dislikes is a most difficult form of worship requiring energy and power to control and restrain the self from inappropriate actions or speech. The servant of Allah is guided by the torch of patience to the wisest course of action.

On the Day of Judgement the Qur'ān will argue in favor of those who recited it and lived by it, and it will testify against those who ignored it and those who recited it but did not live by it. Several ḥadīths mention the intercession of the Qur'ān on behalf of its people.

The final statement compares each day of one's life to a business transaction. Every person expends his efforts for something in return, and through his deeds and intentions he will reap either profit or loss. Some exert their efforts for Allah in exchange for salvation, while others exert them for Shayṭān and thereby obtain punishment in the Hereafter.

Ḥadīth No. 24

عن أبي ذر الغفاري عن النبي (ﷺ) فيما يرويه عن ربه عز وجل أنه قال:

«يَا عِبَادِي: إِنِّي حَرَّمْتُ الظُّلْمَ عَلَى نَفْسِي وَجَعَلْتُهُ بَيْنَكُمْ مُحَرَّمًا فَلاَ تَظَالَمُوا. يَا عِبَادِي: كُلُّكُمْ ضَالٌّ إِلاَّ مَنْ هَدَيْتُهُ فَاسْتَهْدُونِي أَهْدِكُمْ. يَا عِبَادِي: كُلُّكُمْ جَائِعٌ إِلاَّ مَنْ أَطْعَمْتُهُ فَاسْتَطْعِمُونِي أُطْعِمْكُمْ. يَا عِبَادِي: كُلُّكُمْ عَارٍ إِلاَّ مَنْ كَسَوْتُهُ فَاسْتَكْسُونِي أَكْسُكُمْ. يَا عِبَادِي: إِنَّكُمْ تُخْطِئُونَ بِاللَّيْلِ وَالنَّهَارِ، وَأَنَا أَغْفِرُ الذُّنُوبَ جَمِيعًا، فَاسْتَغْفِرُونِي أَغْفِرْ لَكُمْ. يَا عِبَادِي: إِنَّكُمْ لَنْ تَبْلُغُوا ضُرِّي فَتَضُرُّونِي، وَلَنْ تَبْلُغُوا نَفْعِي فَتَنْفَعُونِي. يَا عِبَادِي: لَوْ أَنَّ أَوَّلَكُمْ وَآخِرَكُمْ وَإِنْسَكُمْ وَجِنَّكُمْ كَانُوا عَلَى أَتْقَى قَلْبِ رَجُلٍ وَاحِدٍ مِنْكُمْ، مَا زَادَ ذَلِكَ فِي مُلْكِي شَيْئًا. يَا عِبَادِي: لَوْ أَنَّ أَوَّلَكُمْ وَآخِرَكُمْ وَإِنْسَكُمْ وَجِنَّكُمْ كَانُوا عَلَى أَفْجَرِ قَلْبِ رَجُلٍ وَاحِدٍ مِنْكُمْ، مَا نَقَصَ ذَلِكَ مِنْ مُلْكِي شَيْئًا. يَا عِبَادِي: لَوْ أَنَّ أَوَّلَكُمْ وَآخِرَكُمْ وَإِنْسَكُمْ وَجِنَّكُمْ قَامُوا فِي صَعِيدٍ وَاحِدٍ، فَسَأَلُونِي، فَأَعْطَيْتُ كُلَّ وَاحِدٍ مَسْأَلَتَهُ، مَا نَقَصَ ذَلِكَ مِمَّا عِنْدِي إِلاَّ كَمَا يَنْقُصُ الْمِخْيَطُ إِذَا أُدْخِلَ الْبَحْرَ. يَا عِبَادِي: إِنَّمَا هِيَ أَعْمَالُكُمْ أُحْصِيهَا لَكُمْ، ثُمَّ أُوَفِّيكُمْ إِيَّاهَا فَمَنْ وَجَدَ خَيْرًا فَلْيَحْمَدِ اللهَ، وَمَنْ وَجَدَ غَيْرَ ذَلِكَ فَلاَ يَلُومَنَّ إِلاَّ نَفْسَهُ»

On the authority of Abū Dharr al-Ghifārī from the Prophet (ﷺ) among that which he related from his Lord, the Mighty and Majestic, is that He said:[121]

"O My servants, indeed I have prohibited injustice for Myself and made it among you prohibited, so be not unjust to one another. O My servants, all of you are lost except whom I have guided, so seek guidance from Me and I will guide you. O My servants, all of you are hungry except whom I have fed, so ask Me for food and I will feed you. O My servants, all of you are naked except whom I have clothed, so ask Me for clothing and I will clothe you. O My servants, indeed you err by night and by day and I forgive all sins, so seek forgiveness of Me and I will forgive you. O My servants, never will you reach [so far as] to harm Me so you could harm Me, and never will you reach [so far as] to benefit Me so you could benefit Me. O My servants, if the first of you, the last of you, the humans of you, and the jinn of you were [all] as righteous as the most righteous heart of one man among you, it would not increase My dominion at all. O My servants, if the first of you, the last of you, the humans of you, and the jinn of you were as wicked as the most wicked heart of one man among you, it would not decrease My dominion at all. O My servants, if the first of you, the last of you, the humans of you, and the jinn of you were to stand in one place and ask something of Me and I gave each one his request, that would not decrease what I have except like the needle decreases [the water] when put into the sea. O My servants, it is only your deeds I enumerate for you and then I fully compensate you for them. So whoever finds good – let him praise Allah, and whoever finds otherwise should certainly not blame except himself."

(Narrated by Muslim)

In describing the importance of this ḥadīth, scholars have observed that around it revolves Islam, for it deals with major aspects of belief and practice. In it Allah

---

[121] This is a *ḥadīth qudsi*, i.e., one in which the Prophet (ﷺ) reported what was taught to him by Allah. It is narrated in his own words as opposed to the Qur'ān, which is the wording of Allah Himself.

(*subḥānahu wa ta'ālā*) informs His servants about Himself and directs them toward proper attitudes and behavior.

Since Allah states that He has prohibited Himself from injustice, it becomes clear that He has the ability to do otherwise, but out of His favor, generosity and mercy to His creatures, He willed upon Himself the attribute of justice,[122] which is one aspect of His perfection. Thus, divine injustice is an impossibility, and the believer accepts His laws and His decrees with that knowledge. *Thulm* (injustice, oppression, wrong) has been defined as "putting things in the wrong place," an imperfection from which Allah (*subḥānahu wa ta'ālā*) is naturally disassociated and far removed. And those who interpret it as "the administration of someone's property without his permission" point out additionally that divine injustice is an impossibility because all creation is within the dominion of Allah, wherein He has the right to do as He pleases. It applies equally to His decrees concerning the individual lives of His servants and the fate of nations.

Just as Allah (*subḥānahu wa ta'ālā*) refuses injustice for Himself, He has forbidden it to His servants. The greatest injustice is that which is done to Allah through *shirk* (association of another with Him in some aspect of divinity).[123] This is the sin which severs the relationship between the offender and his Lord, opens the door to every other injustice, and without repentance will not be forgiven.[124] Disobedience to Allah by transgression against others has been described in the Qur'ān as injustice to one's self, since it is the transgressor who will pay the price in the Hereafter. It is condemned in the strongest terms by Allah in the Qur'ān and by His Messenger (ﷺ), who said, "*Injustice is darknesses on the Day of Resurrection,*"[125] and warned, "*Whoever has been unjust to his brother concerning his reputation or anything, let him make a settlement with him over it before [the time when] there will be no dinār or dirham. If he has done any good work, it will be taken from him to the extent of his injustice against the other; and if he has no good deeds, some of his companion's bad deeds will be taken and placed upon him.*"[126] And he (ﷺ) said, "*Indeed, Allah allows time for the transgressor until, when He seizes him, He will not let him escape.*" Then he recited,

وَكَذَٰلِكَ أَخذُ رَبِّكَ إِذَا أَخَذَ الْقُرَىٰ وَهِىَ ظَالِمَةٌ إِنَّ أَخْذَهُ أَلِيمٌ شَدِيدٌ

"*And thus is the seizure of your Lord when He seizes the cities while they are committing injustice. Indeed, His seizure is painful and severe.*"[127]

The second part of the ḥadīth points to the fact that all creatures are in themselves helpless and dependent upon Allah to bring them benefit and protect them from harm, both in this world and the next. For without guidance and provision, man is deprived upon the earth, and without forgiveness he will be deprived in the Hereafter. It also shows that Allah likes supplication from His servants and responds to it, as He says in the Qur'ān:

---

122 Just as He has decreed upon Himself mercy (Sūrah al-An'ām, 6:54). Many verses of the Qur'ān also confirm that Allah is never unjust.

123 إِنَّ الشِّرْكَ لَظُلْمٌ عَظِيم "*Indeed, shirk is a great injustice.*" (Sūrah Luqmān, 31:13)

124 إِنَّ اللَّهَ لاَ يَغفِرُ أَن يُشرَكَ بِهِ وَيَغفِرُ مَا دُونَ ذَٰلِكَ لِمَن يَشَاء "*Indeed, Allah does not forgive that anything be associated with Him, but He forgives what is less than that for whom He wills.*" (Sūrah an-Nisaa', 4:48 and 116)

125 Narrated by al-Bukhāri and Muslim.

126 Narrated by al-Bukhāri.

127 Narrated by Muslim. The Qur'ānic reference is Sūrah Hūd, 11:102.

ادعُونِي أَستَجِب لَكُم

"Call upon Me; I will answer you."[128]

Supplication may be made at any time and for any need, worldly or spiritual, great or small. It is especially encouraged during prostration in prayer,[129] within the last portion of the night, throughout the month of Ramadhān, and on the Day of 'Arafah but is also likely to be answered whenever there is urgency, as long as the supplicant avoids what Allah has forbidden.[130] Further, there is a suggestion that those who have been blessed with guidance and provision should be grateful to Allah, and those in need of them should know that He is the ultimate source and that none can help them without His permission and support.

The meaning of *dhaall* (lost or astray) in relation to man has been given as "ignorant" or "without knowledge." For although every human being is born with a natural inclination towards Islam, actual knowledge of it is necessary for conscious acceptance. Likewise, additional and continued guidance is necessary throughout one's life on earth, as is food and clothing.

Repentance to Allah and seeking His forgiveness is a continuous Islamic obligation[131] because of the fact that despite one's best intentions, he inevitably sins or errs by night and by day. As stated in another ḥadīth, "Each of the children of Adam is a constant sinner, but the best of sinners are the continually repentant."[132] Although protected by Allah from falling into sin, several narrations confirm that the Prophet himself (ﷺ) used to ask forgiveness of Allah for minor faults and errors at least a hundred times each day. In the Qur'ān Allah promises acceptance of true repentance, the conditions of which are:

1) Sincere regret over what was done
2) Determination never to repeat it again
3) Restoration of the rights of injured parties whenever possible
4) Seeking Allah's forgiveness through supplication and the performance of good deeds.

Then Allah (*subḥānahu wa ta'ālā*) reminds His servants that by no means can they ever touch Him with the slightest harm or benefit. And how could they when He is beyond their reach, beyond their sight and senses, exalted above all creation? Moreover, anything they do of good or evil can have no effect upon Him because He is independent of them, and His dominion, as He has willed it, is complete and cannot be increased or decreased. Rather, the righteousness or wickedness stemming from their hearts will affect only their own souls.

Proceeding a step further, it is stated that even if Allah Himself willed to give everything requested by all of His servants at once, it would not decrease His dominion

128 Sūrah Ghāfir, 40:60.
129 Both obligatory and voluntary prayers.
130 Refer to ḥadīth No. 10.
131 As ordered in Sūrah at-Taḥreem, 66:8 and elsewhere in the Qur'ān.
132 Narrated by Aḥmad, at-Tirmidhi, Ibn Mājah and al-Ḥākim – *ḥasan*.

in the least, any more than dipping a needle into the sea decreases its volume. The secret of that lies in His ability to create anything at any time without delay, limitation or failure, according to innumerable possibilities. Therefore, one should not refrain from asking Allah for everything good pertaining to this life and the next, as He is never unwilling to give and does so freely in accordance with His knowledge of what is best.

And finally, Allah (*subḥānahu wa ta`ālā*) weighs and evaluates every deed and repays every expenditure of effort. Full and complete compensation will only be obtained in the Hereafter, although one may see a partial result of his action in this world as well. Praise and gratitude are due to Allah for enabling the righteous servant to achieve righteousness. When such a one finds pain and unpleasant experiences in life, he recognizes them as expiations for his sins which relieve him of their burden before the time of judgement. As the Prophet (ﷺ) told Sa`d bin Abī Waqqāṣ, "*Indeed, afflictions remain with the servant until he walks upon the earth having no sin left on him.*"[133] But when one fails to attain righteousness, having turned away from his Lord, preferring his own inclinations and taking Shayṭān as a companion instead, he cannot then blame Allah, the Exalted, who provided him with hearing, sight and intellect and then sent him ample guidance as a mercy from Himself. Having refused Allah's mercy to him, he will surely blame himself with bitter regret in the Hereafter when he becomes aware of his manifest loss. A believer will also regret what good he neglected in worldly life, therefore, let each one hasten to good deeds so as not to blame himself tomorrow.

---

133 Portion of a ḥadīth narrated by at-Tirmidhi, who graded it *ḥasan-ṣaḥeeḥ*.

Ḥadīth No. 25

عن أبي ذر أيضا:

أَنَّ نَاسًا مِن أَصحَابِ رَسُولِ اللهِ (ﷺ) قَالُوا لِلنَّبِيِّ صَلَّى اللهُ تَعَالَى عَلَيهِ وَسَلَّمَ: يَا رَسُولَ اللهِ، ذَهَبَ أَهلُ الدُّثُورِ بِالأُجُورِ، يُصَلُّونَ كَمَا نُصَلِّي، وَيَصُومُونَ كَمَا نَصُومُ، وَيَصَدَّقُونَ بِفُضُولِ أَموَالِهِم. قَالَ: « أَوَلَيسَ قَد جَعَلَ اللهُ لَكُم مَا تَصَدَّقُونَ؟ إِنَّ بِكُلِّ تَسبِيحَةٍ صَدَقَةً، وَكُلِّ تَكبِيرَةٍ صَدَقَةً، وَكُلِّ تَحمِيدَةٍ صَدَقَةً، وَكُلِّ تَهلِيلَةٍ صَدَقَةً، وَأَمرِ بِالمَعرُوفِ صَدَقَةً، وَنَهيِ عَن مُنكَرٍ صَدَقَةً، وَفِي بُضعِ أَحَدِكُم صَدَقَةً» قَالُوا: يَا رَسُولَ اللهِ أَيَأتِي أَحَدُنَا شَهوَتَهُ وَيَكُونُ لَهُ فِيهَا أَجرٌ؟ قَالَ: « أَرَأَيتُم لَو وَضَعَهَا فِي حَرَامٍ، أَكَانَ عَلَيهِ وِزرٌ؟ فَكَذَلِكَ إِذَا وَضَعَهَا فِي الحَلَالِ كَانَ لَهُ أَجرٌ»

Also on the authority of Abū Dharr:

Some of the companions of the Messenger of Allah said to the Prophet (ﷺ): "O Messenger of Allah, the affluent have taken the rewards: they pray as we pray, they fast as we fast, and they give in charity the excess of their wealth." He said, "Has not Allah made something for you to do in charity? Indeed, in each saying of '*subḥān Allāh*' is a charity, and each '*Allāhu akbar*' is a charity, and each '*al-ḥamdulillāh*' is a charity, and each '*lā ilāha ill-Allāh*' is a charity, and enjoining what is right is a charity, and prohibiting what is wrong is a charity, and in the sexual intercourse of one of you is a charity." They said, "O Messenger of Allah, does one of us indulge in his desire and get for it a reward?" He said, "Have you considered: if he were to do it unlawfully, would he have for it a burden [of sin]? Similarly, when he does it lawfully, he will have for it a reward."

(Narrated by Muslim)

This ḥadīth contains an illustration of the eagerness of the *ṣaḥābah* to perform deeds that would earn Allah's pleasure and reward. It was often evident in the amiable competition among them and their sadness when circumstances prevented them from accomplishing all they desired. Here, the poorer of the Prophet's companions complained to him of their inability to give charities, which they assumed had put them at a disadvantage in the race for Paradise.

The Prophet (ﷺ) therefore directed them and those after them to other kinds of deeds, not requiring material wealth, by which people can earn rewards. He also corrected their understanding of the concept of *ṣadaqah* (charity), redefining it in its true and comprehensive sense. As he stated on another occasion, "Every good deed is a *ṣadaqah*."[134] Among them are deeds which benefit the person himself, such as the remembrance and mention of Allah, and those which benefit others as well, such as the offering of good advice.

Thus, the concept of charity, like that of worship, is not a limited one. This point is emphasized further by the Prophet's mention of a natural act usually associated with pleasure. For one might imagine that the sexual act is unrelated to matters of religion, whereas Islam leaves no aspect of behavior untouched. Every act is either permissible (and possibly obligatory) or prohibited, and reward in the Hereafter depends upon the

---

134 Related by Muslim.

measure of obedience to Allah in each matter. So when one intends through marital intercourse to satisfy himself and his spouse so that they will not be attracted to unlawful relationships or seeks through it a righteous child or any other lawful benefit, he is obeying Allah and can expect His reward. The same applies to any permissible act which, through proper intention, becomes an act of worship.[135] This is how the Muslim becomes a worshipper throughout his life, fulfilling the role Allah meant for him when He said:

وَمَا خَلَقْتُ الجِنَّ وَالإِنسَ إِلاَّ لِيَعْبُدُونِ

"And I did not create the jinn and mankind except to worship Me."[136]

Conversely, if the same act were to be performed in a way disobedient to Allah, punishment could be expected accordingly. The clear balance of divine justice is shown by this example,[137] and in fact, rewards are far in excess of what is deserved by the obedient servant.

---

135 This is true of all such ordinary activities as eating and recreation, where one seeks what is lawful with the intention of strengthening himself for the best performance of his duties.

136 Sūrah adh-Dhāriyāt, 51:56.

137 It also refutes the assertion by supporters of Shayṭān that Islam is largely based upon prohibitions and threats of punishment.

Ḥadīth No. 26

عن أبي هريرة قال: قال رسول الله (ﷺ):

«كُلُّ سُلاَمَى مِنَ النَّاسِ عَلَيهِ صَدَقَةٌ كُلَّ يَومٍ تَطلُعُ فِيهِ الشَّمسُ. تَعدِلُ بَينَ اثنَينِ صَدَقَةٌ، وَتُعِينُ الرَّجُلَ فِي دَابَّتِهِ فَتَحمِلُهُ عَلَيهَا أَو تَرفَعُ لَهُ عَلَيهَا مَتَاعَهُ صَدَقَةٌ، وَالكَلِمَةُ الطَّيِّبَةُ صَدَقَةٌ، وَبِكُلِّ خَطوَةٍ تَمشِيهَا إِلَى الصَّلاَةِ صَدَقَةٌ، وَتُمِيطُ الأَذَى عَنِ الطَّرِيقِ صَدَقَةٌ»

On the authority of Abū Hurayrah, who said: The Messenger of Allah (ﷺ) said:

"Upon the people's every joint a charity is due each day the sun rises. Your being just between two persons is a charity; your helping a man with his mount, lifting him onto it or hoisting up his belongings onto it for him is a charity; and a good word is a charity. And with each step you take walking to the [congregational] prayer is a charity; and your removing something harmful from the road is a charity."

(Narrated by al-Bukhāri and Muslim)

The word "*sulāmā*" was used originally in reference to the smallest bones in a camel's skeleton or to the bones and joints of the human hand and foot. The term later became generalized to include all bones of the body. The precise assembly of bones and joints into a mobile structure supporting the whole body is one of the greatest blessings from Allah for which the servant should be constantly grateful.[138] It is obvious that any dysfunction or damage to a small bone in the body would cause great pain and disability, yet how often does a healthy person remember this favor?

Hence, the Prophet (ﷺ) has reminded Muslims to be grateful daily for the health and mobility given them by Allah (*subḥānahu wa ta'ālā*) and that upon the body is a form of *zakāh,* just as there is upon wealth – the *zakāh* of the body being the performance of righteous deeds. This has been confirmed in several similar narratives as well. A few scholars have stated that the *ṣadaqah* (charity) of this type is a voluntary one but that gratitude is due to Allah from every servant, if only in the heart, while deeds are evidence of recognition and gratitude. Others have pointed out that the minimum due to Allah is performance of obligatory duties and refraining from disobedience, and these are among the "charities" named by the Prophet (ﷺ) in various ḥadīths.

In this ḥadīth, again, by giving a few examples, Allah's Messenger (ﷺ) emphasizes that all kinds of good deeds are charities acceptable to Allah. The deeds listed here differ from those in the previous ḥadīth, and indeed, each narration is a variation, illustrating diversity in the possibilities for *ṣadaqah* according to one's ability and circumstance. In addition to his duty to Allah, they include obligations to fellow men, good conduct, all kinds of assistance, a pleasant manner, and even, as narrated by al-Bukhāri and Muslim, refraining from evil and sparing the people from that.

The Prophet (ﷺ) has also been reported to have said, "*And what serves in place of all that [i.e., good works when unable to perform them] is two rak`ahs of the dhuḥā*

---

138 The skeletal framework also serves to protect such organs as the heart, lungs and brain. It has the property of repairing itself when broken or fractured.

prayer."¹³⁹ Scholars have speculated that this may be because prayer involves the entire body, including its every bone and joint, but Allah knows best.

Ḥadīth No. 27

عن النواس بن سمعان عن النبي (ﷺ) قال:

«البِرُّ حُسْنُ الخُلُقِ، وَالإِثْمُ مَا حَاكَ فِي نَفْسِكَ وَكَرِهْتَ أَنْ يَطَّلِعَ عَلَيْهِ النَّاسُ.»

On the authority of an-Nawwās bin Samʿān that the Prophet (ﷺ) said:

"Righteousness is good morals, and wrongdoing is that which wavers within yourself and you would dislike people to discover."

(Narrated by Muslim)

وعن وابصة بن معبد قال:

أَتَيْتُ رَسُولَ اللهِ (ﷺ) فَقَالَ: «جِئْتَ تَسْأَلُ عَنِ البِرِّ؟» قُلْتُ: نَعَم. قَالَ: «اسْتَفْتِ قَلْبَكَ، البِرُّ مَا اطْمَأَنَّتْ إِلَيْهِ النَّفْسُ وَاطْمَأَنَّ إِلَيْهِ القَلْبُ، وَالإِثْمُ مَا حَاكَ فِي النَّفْسِ وَتَرَدَّدَ فِي الصَّدْرِ وَإِنْ أَفْتَاكَ النَّاسُ وَأَفْتَوْكَ.»

On the authority of Wābiṣah bin Maʿbad, who said:

I came to the Messenger of Allah (ﷺ), and he said, "You have come to ask about righteousness?" I said, "Yes." He said, "Consult your heart. Righteousness is that with which the self is assured and the heart is assured, and wrongdoing is that which wavers within the self and falters in the breast, even if the people have given you a ruling and gave you a ruling [again]."

(Narrated in the *Musnads* of the two Imāms, Aḥmad bin Ḥanbal and ad-Dārimi - *ḥasan*)

Here, al-Imām an-Nawawi has chosen two ḥadīths which are similar in wording and in meaning. The subject of doubt was also dealt with in Ḥadīth No. 6 and No. 11, but this time an additional point has been made, which is that the heart of the righteous believer who fears Allah and is illuminated by His light is able to discern truth from falsehood and right from wrong. When measured against the standard given by the Prophet (ﷺ) in these two ḥadīths, the believer will be able to make his own decisions about many matters without relying on a *fatwa* (legal ruling), especially at times when a scholar of comprehensive knowledge and true sincerity cannot be easily found.

Righteousness (*al-birr*) has been defined by Allah (*subḥānahu wa taʿālā*) in the Qur'ān¹⁴⁰ as correct belief, assistance to others with one's excess wealth, regular performance of prayer, giving due *zakāh*, fulfilling one's promises, and patience in the face of difficulties. All of this is included in the Prophet's definition, "*Righteousness is good morals*," which means obedience to Allah and every kind of correct behavior based

---

139 Narrated by Aḥmad, Muslim and Abū Dāwūd.
140 See Sūrah al-Baqarah, 2:177.

on the teachings of the Qur'ān and *sunnah,* such as fairness in dealings, gentleness in persuasion, and efforts toward *iḥsān.* The descriptions of true believers throughout the Qur'ān show the qualities approved by Allah and considered to be those of righteousness. Anyone who wonders about his own condition may compare himself with those descriptions and then work to attain what is lacking in him.

In contrast, wrongdoing or sin is that which is distasteful to a believer and which he would strive to avoid. But how does he perceive whether or not a specific act is sinful? The Prophet's answer was that when carefully considered, a wrong or sinful option will put the believer into a state of discomfort and uneasiness, for he knows that Allah is fully aware of his intentions and motives. Another way to evaluate an intent is to imagine the probable reaction of one's associates[141] if they should know about it. That is because humans are prone to criticize each other, while the self, aided by Shayṭān, usually attempts to justify its own inclinations. So if one feels he would be censured by people for whatever he is contemplating and would not wish them to be aware of it, he will conclude that it must be blameworthy.

Similarly, the heart of a true believer will not accept every *fatwā* without reservation, and especially opinions not supported by evidence from the Qur'ān or *sunnah.* He will be wary of allowances made for the sake of preference alone. He will not be moved by the large numbers of ignorant or less than pious people who are quick to offer a *fatwa* on every occasion. These are most unlike the true scholar,[142] who is often reluctant to do so out of fear of Allah. The recurrence and repetition of such rulings will not sway the believer who walks in the light of Allah, and he will never feel confident or reassured by them. For in the end, it is he who will have to stand with his decision before Allah on the Day when the truth of every matter is exposed.

---

141 i.e., believers like himself. Scholars have pointed out that "people" in this ḥadīth does not refer to the base and ignoble among them but rather to those whose standard for conduct is the Islamic *Shari`ah.*

142 A qualified *mufti* (one who issues legal rulings) will not only have a vast knowledge and adequate understanding of the *Shari`ah* but also of the circumstances in which people are living in order to assess their needs when reviewing feasible options within the law. He will be aware of the possible consequences, both positive and negative, of his ruling, while always fearing Allah's judgement of himself. Once satisfied regarding the comprehensiveness of a particular *mufti's* knowledge and his trustworthiness, the believer's heart would normally be receptive to his *fatwā.*

Ḥadīth No. 28

عن أبي نجيح العرباض بن سارية قال:

وَعَظَنَا رَسُولُ اللهِ (ﷺ) مَوْعِظَةً وَجِلَتْ مِنْهَا الْقُلُوبُ وَذَرَفَتْ مِنْهَا الْعُيُونُ، فَقُلْنَا: يَا رَسُولَ اللهِ، كَأَنَّهَا مَوْعِظَةُ مُوَدِّعٍ، فَأَوْصِنَا. قَالَ: «أُوصِيكُمْ بِتَقْوَى اللهِ عَزَّ وَجَلَّ، وَالسَّمْعِ وَالطَّاعَةِ وَإِنْ تَأَمَّرَ عَلَيْكُمْ عَبْدٌ فَإِنَّهُ مَنْ يَعِشْ مِنْكُمْ فَسَيَرَى اخْتِلَافًا كَثِيرًا. فَعَلَيْكُمْ بِسُنَّتِي وَسُنَّةِ الْخُلَفَاءِ الرَّاشِدِينَ الْمَهْدِيِّينَ، عَضُّوا عَلَيْهَا بِالنَّوَاجِذِ وَإِيَّاكُمْ وَمُحْدَثَاتِ الْأُمُورِ فَإِنَّ كُلَّ مُحْدَثَةٍ بِدْعَةٌ وَكُلَّ بِدْعَةٍ ضَلَالَةٌ، وَكُلَّ ضَلَالَةٍ فِي النَّارِ».

On the authority of Abū Najeeḥ al-'Irbādh bin Sāriyah, who said:

The Messenger of Allah (ﷺ) admonished us with a warning from which [our] hearts became fearful and [our] eyes shed tears. So we said, "O Messenger of Allah (ﷺ), it is as if it was a final warning, so instruct us." He said, "I direct you to fear Allah, the Mighty and Majestic, and to hear and obey, even if a slave is made a leader over you. For indeed, he who lives long among you will see much controversy. So you must adhere to my sunnah and the sunnah of the rightly guided caliphs; clench it with your molar teeth. And beware of newly devised matters, for every newly devised thing is an innovation, and every innovation is misguidance, and every misguidance is in the Fire."

(Narrated by Abū Dāwūd and at-Tirmidhi who graded it *ḥasan-ṣaḥeeḥ*)

In another narration by Aḥmad, Abū Dāwūd and at-Tirmidhi, it is reported that the Prophet's speech on this occasion was given following the *fajr* (dawn) prayer. He (ﷺ) often used to counsel his companions at times other than the Friday *khuṭbah*; yet not so often as to tire or bore them. His words were eloquent, short and to the point. Even during the *Jumu`ah* sermon, he preferred to keep the *khuṭbah* short and lengthen the prayer. The period for the *khuṭbah* was subsequently increased due to the fact that many people no longer hear such reminders and warnings except when they attend the Friday prayer.

On this particular day they had been shaken by the warnings. The fear and apprehension they felt was that of true believers as described by Allah in the Qur'ān.[143] The forcefulness of the admonition suggested to the listeners that possibly there would be no more, so they requested advice or instruction upon which they could rely thereafter. The Prophet (ﷺ) replied, "*I direct you to fear Allah*," for *taqwā*[144] is the key to happiness in the Hereafter. Therefore, Allah (subḥānahu wa ta`ālā) has enjoined it upon His servants in every age and said:

وَلَقَدْ وَصَّيْنَا الَّذِينَ أُوتُوا الْكِتَابَ مِن قَبْلِكُمْ وَإِيَّاكُمْ أَنِ اتَّقُوا اللهَ

"And We have instructed those who were given the Scripture before you and yourselves to fear Allah."[145]

Then the Messenger of Allah (ﷺ) continued, "*and to hear and obey*," meaning obedience to the Muslim ruler, whose duty it is to amend and regulate the life of the

---

143 See verses 8:2, 22:34-35, 39:23 and 57:16.
144 An explanation of *taqwā* is found in Ḥadīth No. 18.
145 Sūrah an-Nisaa', 4:131.

community, serve public interest, and facilitate the worship of Allah. Obedience is due even to a corrupt ruler as long as his order involves no disobedience to Allah or His Messenger, and patience is urged in the face of what is distasteful.[146] The words "even if a slave is made a leader over you" have been interpreted by some as an allusion to a most unlikely situation, since a slave cannot hold such a position, he himself being owned by another person. Others have speculated that this may refer to a corrupt period in which people are ruled by those without proper qualification. When that happens, the Muslims are advised to obey them and show forbearance in order to avoid the greater calamity of dissension and civil strife among themselves. A further inference is that the Muslim ruler should be obeyed without any reservation concerning his origin, for it is possible that an Imām from Quraysh[147] could appoint a slave as a regional governor who would be answerable to him.

The Prophet (ﷺ) then warned of future dissensions, giving an instruction which would prevent the Muslim from losing himself in the chaos of the many opinions and assertions concerning the religion prevalent at that time: "*You must adhere to my sunnah and the sunnah of the rightly guided caliphs; clench it with your molar teeth.*"[148] "Sunnah" is defined linguistically as "a way or course followed repeatedly or habitually," and in Islamic terminology as "that way practiced or advocated by the Prophet (ﷺ) and his four successors, Abū Bakr, 'Umar, 'Uthmān and 'Ali." This was understood by the *salaf* (earliest Islamic scholars) to be the complete sunnah, and it includes beliefs, sayings and deeds. The Prophet's emphasis on adherence to the sunnah following his order to obey Muslim rulers serves to limit the concept of obedience and define what is obligatory in that regard.

"*Beware of newly devised matters*" refers to those pertaining to the religion of Islam and does not include everyday worldly affairs. New inventions and discoveries by man which serve his interests outside the realm of religion are permissible as long as they are not specifically prohibited in the Qur'ān or sunnah or are known to be harmful.

The word "*bid`ah*" is defined linguistically as "origination," or the bringing into existence of something new without a previous pattern or model. Hence, it means an innovation, invention or novelty. Islamically, it is that which has no basis in the *sharī'ah,* the antithesis of *sunnah.* The statement "*every bid`ah [innovation] is misguidance*" shows that it is unacceptable and outside the ordained religion of Allah. Again, this does not mean public interest rulings within the framework of *Sharī`ah,* which were sometimes called "*bid`ah*" in the linguistic sense only. But it certainly includes the deviations of those sects which broke away from *Ahl as-Sunnah* – their false doctrines and assertions concerning faith, deeds and their outcome, and worse, concerning the attributes of Allah. And it includes any act of worship claimed to be a means of approaching Allah or obtaining His reward that was not taught by His Messenger (ﷺ), who warned clearly against misguidance and its evil result.

146 Several authentic ḥadīths emphasize that obedience is limited to what is lawful and reasonable, such as this one narrated by al-Bukhāri and Muslim: "There is no obedience to anyone in disobedience to Allah. Obedience is only in what is right."

147Several ḥadīths state that leadership of the *ummah* will remain with the Quraysh.

148i.e., hold on to it firmly.

Hadīth No. 29

عن معاذ بن جبل قال:

قُلتُ: يَارَسُولَ اللهِ، أَخبِرنِي بِعَمَلٍ يُدخِلُنِي الجَنَّةَ، وَيُبَاعِدُنِي عَنِ النَّارِ، قَالَ: «لَقَد سَأَلتَ عَن عَظِيمٍ، وَإِنَّهُ لَيَسِيرٌ عَلَى مَن يَسرَّهُ اللهُ تَعَالَى عَلَيهِ: تَعبُدُ اللهَ لاَ تُشرِكُ بِهِ شَيئًا، وَتُقِيمُ الصَّلاَةَ، وَتُؤتِي الزَّكَاةَ، وَتَصُومُ رَمَضَانَ، وَتَحُجُّ البَيتَ.» ثُمَّ قَالَ: « أَلاَ أَدُلُّكَ عَلَى أَبوَابِ الخَيرِ: الصَّومُ جُنَّةٌ، وَالصَّدَقَةُ تُطفِئُ الخَطِيئَةَ كَمَا يُطفِئُ المَاءُ النَّارَ، وَصَلاَةُ الرَّجُلِ فِي جَوفِ اللَّيلِ، ثُمَّ تَلاَ: تَتَجَافَى جُنُوبُهُم عَنِ المَضَاجِعِ حَتَّى بَلَغَ يَعمَلُونَ» ثُمَّ قَالَ: « أَلاَ أُخبِرُكَ بِرَأسِ الأَمرِ وَعَمُودِهِ وَذِروَةِ سَنَامِهِ؟» قُلتُ: بَلَى يَارَسُولَ اللهِ. قَالَ: « رَأسُ الأَمرِ الإِسلاَمُ، وَعَمُودُهُ الصَّلاَةُ، وَذِروَةُ سَنَامِهِ الجِهَادُ» ثُمَّ قَالَ: «أَلاَ أُخبِرُكَ بِمِلاَكِ ذَلِكَ كُلِّهِ؟» قُلتُ: بَلَى يَارَسُولَ اللهِ، فَأَخَذَ بِلِسَانِهِ وَقَالَ: «كُفَّ عَلَيكَ هَذَا» قُلتُ: يَانَبِيَّ اللهِ، وَإِنَّا لَمُؤاخَذُونَ بِمَا نَتَكَلَّمُ بِهِ؟ فَقَالَ: «ثَكِلَتكَ أُمُّكَ يَا مُعَاذُ، وَهَل يَكُبُّ النَّاسَ فِي النَّارِ عَلَى وَجُوهِهِم – أَو قَالَ: عَلَى مَنَاخِرِهِم – إِلاَّ حَصَائِدُ أَلسِنَتِهِم؟»

On the authority of Mu'ādh bin Jabal, who said:

I said, "O Messenger of Allah (ﷺ), inform me of a deed which will take me into Paradise and keep me away from the Fire." He said, "You have asked me about a tremendous matter, but indeed, it is easy for one for whom Allah, the Exalted, makes it easy. You should worship Allah, associating nothing with Him, establish prayer, fast [the month of] Ramadhān, and make the pilgrimage to the House."[149] Then he said, "Shall I not point out to you the gates of goodness? Fasting is a shield. Charity extinguishes sin as water extinguishes fire and [so does] the prayer of a man in the middle of the night." Then he recited: ***"They forsake their beds, invoking their Lord in fear and hope, and spend of that We have provided them. And no soul knows what has been hidden for them of satisfaction as reward for what they used to do."***[150] Then he said, "Shall I not inform you of the head of the matter, its pillar and the peak of its elevation?" I said, "Yes, O Messenger of Allah." He said, "The head of the matter is islām [i.e., submission], its pillar is prayer, and the peak of its elevation is jihād." Then he said, "Shall I not inform you of the foundation of all that?" I said, "Yes, O Messenger of Allah." So he took hold of his tongue and said, "Restrain this." I said, "O Prophet of Allah, will we be blamed for what we talk about?" He said, "May your mother be bereaved of you, O Mu'ādh! Does anything topple people into the Fire on their faces" or he said, "on their noses except the harvests of their tongues?"

(Narrated by at-Tirmidhi, who said it was *ḥasan-ṣaḥeeḥ*)

In answer to the request of Mu'ādh, Allah's Messenger (ﷺ) outlined the important deeds which, when done conscientiously, are a means to attain Paradise through the mercy of Allah and His permission.[151] Preceding his counsel, he conceded that Mu'ādh

---

149 The Ka'bah in Makkah.

150 Sūrah as-Sajdah, 32:16-17.

151 The Prophet's statement, "*None of you will enter Paradise by his deeds*" is understood to mean – and Allah knows best – that human deeds in themselves are inadequate to make one worthy of Paradise, but Allah (*subḥānahu wa ta'ālā*) in His mercy and generosity has made the performance of good

had asked about a crucial and difficult matter but that with Allah's help it becomes easy. Thus, one should ask His assistance in all he undertakes and seek His acceptance of every good deed.

The Prophet (ﷺ) began his list of virtuous deeds with *tawḥeed* (the worship of Allah alone), then recalled the obligatory duties of Islam[152] which lead to Paradise. He followed these with the supplementary acts which draw a person closer to Allah after the fulfillment of his obligations:

- "Fasting is a shield." – This refers to voluntary fasting, as that of Rama<u>dh</u>ān has already been mentioned. Other authentic ḥadīths confirm that fasting is a shield from the Fire, i.e., from disobedient acts which lead one to the Fire. This is perceived when one considers that the Messenger of Allah (ﷺ) warned against sins that can prevent the acceptance of a fast, such as lying, backbiting and evil speech in general. These, as several of the companions noted, perforate the shield, lessening its protection.
- "Charity extinguishes sin," or, as in another narration, "extinguishes the anger of the Lord" – Allah has confirmed in the Qur'ān: إِنَّ الْحَسَنَاتِ يُذْهِبْنَ السَّيِّئَاتِ ***"Indeed, good deeds do away with misdeeds."***[153]
- "The prayer of a man in the middle of the night" – One who foregoes sleep in order to pray and supplicate will not be refused. According to another ḥadīth: "Our Lord descends every night to the lowest heaven when the last third of the night remains and says, 'Who will supplicate to Me so I will respond to him? Who will ask Me so I will give him? Who will seek My forgiveness so I will forgive him?'"[154] The Prophet's recitation of the verses from *Sūrah as-Sajdah* reminds that there is great reward in this practice as well. He himself is known to have performed prayers during various periods of the night: the early part, the middle part and the later part before dawn. And he (ﷺ) said, "The most preferred prayer after the obligatory one is *qiyām al-layl* [voluntary prayer during the night]."[155]

Not content to stop here, the Prophet (ﷺ) continued, "*Shall I not inform you of the head of the matter,*[156] *its pillar and the peak of its elevation?*" Then he explained each of these:

- "The head of the matter is *Islam.*" – In a similar ḥadīth narrated by Aḥmad he was more specific, saying that it is to acknowledge that there is no deity except Allah alone, having no partner, and that Muḥammad (ﷺ) is His servant and messenger. In short, it means acceptance of and concurrence with the final divine message, which entails obedience to Allah's legislation.
- "Its pillar [or backbone] is prayer." – Prayer has always been an essential part of

---

deeds by His righteous servants a cause for their entrance when He accepts and approves of them. Thus, the servant succeeds by Allah's mercy to him and not his deeds alone.

152 As mentioned in Ḥadīths No. 2, No. 3 and No. 22.

153 Sūrah Hūd, 11:114.

154 Narrated by al-Bukhāri, Muslim and others.

155 Narrated by Muslim.

156 The matter, here being the religion. More literally, it has been described metaphorically by the Prophet (ﷺ) as a camel, having a head, a spinal column and a hump.

Allah's religion, practiced by all the prophets and their followers. It has been ordered continuously throughout the Qur'ān and emphasized by the Prophet (ﷺ) as a requisite to faith: "Between a man and disbelief is [only] the abandonment of prayer."[157]

- "The peak of its elevation [or hump] is *jihād*." – From this, al-Imām Aḥmad and other scholars have inferred that *jihād* is the best of deeds after the *farā'iḏh* (obligatory duties). Ḥadīths related by al-Bukhāri and Muslim state that the best deed after belief in Allah (requiring obedience to His ordinances) is *jihād* (i.e., fighting or striving) in His cause. The merits of *jihād* are recounted in numerous narrations and are well known.

Finally, Allah's Messenger (ﷺ) went on to mention *jihād an-nafs,* or striving against the whims and inclinations of one's self,[158] which are utilized by Shayṭān to harm people in their religion and often in their worldly affairs as well. Thus, the Prophet (ﷺ) returned from the summit to the foundation and substance of all goodness: self-control, and in particular, control of the tongue.[159] Restraining the tongue from ill speech is therefore a prerequisite to entering Paradise – something upon which it depends, for the harvest of the tongue is that which it has earned of good or evil, and it will be reaped on the Day of Judgement.

It is to be concluded from this ḥadīth as well that the greatest cause for people entering Hellfire is what they utter with their tongues. For the sin of speech includes *shirk,*[160] which is the worst of sins, and includes other major sins such as false testimony, lying, slander, backbiting, fortunetelling, cursing, insulting and various other transgressions of the tongue, great and small. In addition, most sins committed by the body are accompanied by speech and often preceded by conspiracy. All this was confirmed in concise words by Allah's Messenger (ﷺ) to Mu'ādh, may Allah be pleased with him.

---

157 Narrated by Aḥmad, at-Tirmidhi and an-Nasā'i – *ṣaḥeeḥ*.

158 The frequently quoted saying, "We have returned from the lesser jihād [against disbelief] to the greater jihād [against the self]" is graded as *ḏḥa`eef* (weak) and thus unattributable to the Prophet (ﷺ). Ibn Ḥajar traced it to one of the *tābi'een,* Ibrāheem bin 'Ablah.

159 The subject has also been discussed under Ḥadīths No. 12 and No. 15 of this collection.

160 The association of another with Allah in attributes or worship.

Hadīth No. 30

عن أبي ثعلبة الخشني جرثوم بن ناشر عن رسول الله (ﷺ) قال:

«إِنَّ اللهَ تَعَالَى فَرَضَ فَرَائِضَ فَلاَ تُضَيِّعُوهَا، وَحَدَّ حُدُودًا فَلاَ تَعتَدُوهَا، وَحَرَّمَ أَشيَاءَ فَلاَ تَنتَهِكُوهَا، وَسَكَتَ عَن أَشيَاءَ رَحمَةً لَكُم غَيرَ نِسيَانٍ فَلاَ تَبحَثُوا عَنهَا»

On the authority of Abū Tha'labah al-Khushani, Jurthūm bin Nāshir, that the Messenger of Allah (ﷺ) said:

"Indeed, Allah, the Exalted, has imposed [religious] obligations, so do not neglect them. And He has set limits, so do not overstep them. And He has prohibited things, so do not violate them. And He has kept silent about [certain] things out of mercy to you, not forgetfulness, so do not search them out."

(Ḥadīth *ḥasan* narrated by ad-Daraqutni and others)

This ḥadīth has been described as a great source of the fundamentals of the religion. Several scholars have asserted that among all the ḥadīths of the Messenger of Allah (ﷺ), there is no one ḥadīth more inclusive of the fundamental principles and branches of knowledge than that of Abū Tha'labah. It has divided Allah's rulings into four categories: obligations, prohibitions, limits of permissibility, and what is not mentioned, and these constitute the entire religion. Hence, whoever acts according to this ḥadīth will have obtained reward and escaped penalty.

The obligations (*farā'idh*) are those stipulated by Allah (*subḥānahu wa ta'ālā*) in the Qur'ān or through His Prophet (ﷺ), the denial of which removes one from the fold of Islam. Among them are *fardh `ayn,* or what is obligatory upon every Muslim and cannot be fulfilled by another, and *fardh kifāyah,* or what is obligatory upon specific groups or individuals at specific times; when a sufficient number of qualified people fulfill the obligation, the rest are excused.

The prohibitions (*muḥarramāt*) are also specified in the Qur'ān and sunnah, such as those pertaining to food, marriage, finances, etc. However, there are those things forbidden by the Prophet (ﷺ) which are *ḥarām* by law, and others merely disliked or discouraged by him (*makrūh*), these often pertaining to manners and behavior. There have been differences among scholars over which was intended in certain cases, although the practice of the more piously cautious ones, such as al-Imām Aḥmad, was to avoid a ruling that something was *ḥarām* wherever the slightest doubt existed. They would say, "I disapprove of such an act," but when pressed to declare it *ḥarām,* would adamantly refuse in the absence of a clear proof.

The limits (*ḥudūd*) are the boundaries containing all that is permissible, as Allah and His Messenger (ﷺ) warned against overstepping them into what is unlawful. Additionally, the word "*ḥudūd*" may refer to the prohibited things themselves, as well as to the physical punishments stipulated in the Qur'ān for major crimes. Thus, the phrase in this ḥadīth can also mean: "Do not overstep the bounds in inflicting these punishments," but Allah knows best.

As for things not mentioned, they are those neither stated to be *ḥalāl* nor *ḥarām,* neither encouraged nor discouraged, and these have been overlooked by Allah out of

His mercy. Therefore, there can be no penalty or blame on one who does them and no penalty or blame on one who does not do them. The prohibition against searching them out is said to be of two kinds:

1) A temporary prohibition during the lifetime of the Prophet (ﷺ), out of fear that Allah (*subḥānahu wa ta'ālā*) would rule that a matter in question was unlawful, as He did when the Jews became obstinate in demanding answers of their prophet. Another ḥadīth explains: "*Leave me alone as long as I have left you alone, for those before you were destroyed by their excessive questioning and disagreement with their prophets.*"[161] This is also compatible with Allah's statement in the Qur'ān:

   يَاأَيُّهَا الَّذِينَ آمَنُوا لاَ تَسْئَلُوا عَنْ أَشْيَاءَ إِن تُبْدَ لَكُمْ تَسُؤْكُمْ وَإِن تَسْئَلُوا عَنْهَا حِينَ يُنَزَّلُ الْقُرآنُ تُبْدَلَكُمْ

   "O you who have believed, do not ask about things which, if they are shown to you, will distress you; but if you ask about them while the Qur'ān is being revealed, they will be shown to you."[162]

2) A general prohibition applicable to all times, such as the Prophet's saying: "*Destroyed are the excessive in speech.*"[163] These are persons who persistently continue in futile discussions, delving into irrelevancies and what should not concern them, seeking rulings on matters which Allah has left unmentioned.

The *ṣaḥābah* understood this prohibition well and avoided all unnecessary questioning. Many early scholars thus ruled against asking about anything that had not yet occurred – except that when they feared the loss of knowledge, they began to admit some theoretical situations into their *fiqh* discussions.

The general prohibition includes speculation about those aspects of the unseen which are a required part of a Muslim's faith. One should not try to imagine, much less discuss or research into, how these realities actually exist or what they are like, for this will only lead him to error and eventually disbelief, as illustrated in several ḥadīths of similar wordings: "*People will continue to question until it is said, 'Allah has created creation, so who created Allah?'*"[164] Believers are warned to fear Allah in relation to such issues and limit themselves to the information which Allah (*subḥānahu wa ta'ālā*) has revealed.

161 Narrated by Aḥmad and Muslim.
162 Sūrah al-Mā'idah, 5:101.
163 Narrated by Muslim.
164 Narrated by al-Bukhārī and Muslim.

Ḥadīth No. 31

عن أبي العباس سهل بن سعد الساعدي قال:

«جَاءَ رَجُلٌ إِلَى النَّبِيِّ (ﷺ) فَقَالَ: يَا رَسُولَ اللهِ دُلَّنِي عَلَى عَمَلٍ إِذَا عَمِلْتُهُ أَحَبَّنِي اللهُ، وَأَحَبَّنِي النَّاسُ. فَقَالَ: «ازْهَدْ فِي الدُّنْيَا يُحِبَّكَ اللهُ، وَازْهَدْ فِيمَا عِنْدَ النَّاسِ يُحِبَّكَ النَّاسُ»

On the authority of Abul-'Abbās, Sahl bin Sa'd as-Sā'idi, who said:

A man came to the Prophet (ﷺ) and said, "O Messenger of Allah, direct me to a deed which, when I have done it, Allah will love me and people will love me." So he said, "Be indifferent toward [pleasures of] the world and Allah will love you, and be indifferent toward what people have and people will love you."

(Ḥadīth *hasan* narrated by Ibn Mājah and others with good chains of narrators)

It is well known that the Messenger of Allah (ﷺ) often discouraged excessive concern with those affairs of this world which have no bearing on the Hereafter and encouraged "*zuhd*," which means "indifference" or considering a thing to be small, unimportant or insignificant. In truth, what is of value in worldly life is only that which can serve as a means to Allah's pleasure and reward in the everlasting life to come, for every inhabitant of this earth is but a guest, and whatever he possesses is borrowed. The world's temporary provisions are enjoyed by both the righteous and the wicked, and certain portions are denied to the righteous and some to the wicked, according to Allah's will. The righteous, however, are directed to be content with what He has decreed for them in this life, to use what they have in the best way, and not give undue thought to what they do not possess. This does not mean that a servant of Allah should not exert himself to obtain what he can lawfully for the benefit of himself and others, but only that he must not dwell upon what he cannot obtain, for it is what Allah has decreed. Similarly, worldly misfortunes and disasters, when seen in a proper perspective, lose much of their bitterness and draw the believer nearer to Allah. The Prophet (ﷺ) assured the inquiring companion that an accepting attitude and disregard for worldly pleasure would secure for him the love of Allah, which means His acceptance and approval of him.

The advice given by the Prophet (ﷺ) is not a simple matter, for in fact, mankind is prone to seek immediate pleasures and gratification, as Allah has stated in the Qur'ān:

تُرِيدُونَ عَرَضَ الدُّنْيَا وَاللهُ يُرِيدُ الآخِرَةَ

"You desire the commodities of this world, while Allah desires [for you] the Hereafter."[165]

وَفَرِحُوا بِالْحَيَاةِ الدُّنْيَا وَمَا الْحَيَاةُ الدُّنْيَا فِي الآخِرَةِ إِلَّا مَتَاعٌ

"And they rejoice in the worldly life, and the worldly life is not, compared to the Hereafter, but [brief] enjoyment."[166]

---

165 Sūrah al-Anfāl, 8:67.
166 Sūrah ar-Ra'd, 13:26.

بَل تُؤثِرُونَ الحَيَاةَ الدُّنيَا وَالآخِرَةُ خَيرٌ وَأَبقَى

"But you prefer the worldly life, while the Hereafter is better and more lasting."[167]

Yet, as the Prophet (ﷺ) pointed out, "*If the world in the sight of Allah equaled as much as the wing of a mosquito, He would not have given the disbeliever a drink [of water].*"[168] And he (ﷺ) said, "*The world is not, compared to the Hereafter, but as when one of you dips his finger into the sea; let him see what it brings back.*"[169]

Indifference to the world has been described by scholars as several kinds, among them:

1) That a servant of Allah is more confident of what is in the hand of Allah than what is in his own hand, i.e., he depends upon Allah, knowing that He is the provider and that whatever he owns remains with him only as long as Allah wills. He trusts completely in Allah, accepts His plan in regard to his affairs, and does not fear or place his hope in created beings like himself. He will not seek a benefit through unlawful means, anger Allah seeking to please the people, praise any person for what Allah has provided, or blame any person for what Allah has withheld. All of this results from certainty in faith.

2) That the servant, when struck with a mishap such as the loss of property or death of a child, is more desirous of its reward with Allah than that his loss should be returned to him. This again is due to certainty in faith.

3) That the servant feels the same toward someone who praises him and someone who blames him in the cause of truth. His regard for truth and right, which is pleasing to Allah, exceeds his concern for the world and opinions of other men which affect his standing and position therein. He also considers that others are better than himself and admits it.

4) That the servant has limited hope, i.e., he does not entertain much expectation from the world or plan far into the future but instead places his real hope in the meeting with Allah, and hence, in his exit from this world. His understanding that the purpose of this life is to prepare for the next one leads him to concentrate on what will benefit him there. As illustrated by the Prophet (ﷺ): "*The example of me and the world is like the shade of a tree in which a rider naps at noon; then he moves on and leaves it.*"[170] And he advised Ibn `Umar, "*Be in this world as a stranger or a traveler.*"[171]

Therefore, what one takes from the world should be like the provisions for a journey – only what is needed until he reaches his destination. This means that the servant will not deprive himself of legitimate needs. He will take whatever is necessary to strengthen him for obedience to Allah and can expect to be rewarded for that as well. As Mu'ādh bin Jabal said, "I seek reward for sleeping, just as I seek it for standing

167 Sūrah al-A'lā, 87:16-17.

168 At-Tirmidhi and Ibn Mājah – ṣaḥeeḥ.

169 Narrated by Muslim.

170 Aḥmad and at-Tirmidhi, who graded it ḥasan-ṣaḥeeḥ.

171 Narrated by al-Bukhāri. This ḥadīth is No. 40 of an-Nawawi's collection.

in prayer," meaning that his intention to sleep in order to enable him to worship later in the night will not be overlooked by Allah.[172] Periods of rest from duties and lawful diversions become worship when intended to facilitate the continuation of those duties and other good deeds. Sa`eed bin Jubayr added that not all worldly provisions distract one from seeking the Hereafter; rather, they could be a means to a better position therein. Thus, the lawful things of this world are to be renounced only when they become an end in themselves. Allah (*subḥānahu wa ta'ālā*) will love the servant whose possessions are in his hand to be used, not in his heart to be cherished.

The second part of the Prophet's advice, to be indifferent toward what people possess, is essential to good social relationships. Several ḥadīths advise self-sufficiency and abstention from asking anything of people (or even appearing to wish for it in their presence), thus avoiding humiliation by them and feelings of indebtedness which erode one's honor. For it is known that most human beings dislike and disdain those who seek to take their possessions, and they try to avoid them. The same is true of those who are in the habit of asking unnecessary favors requiring time, effort or certain difficulties.

It may be understood that cases of dire necessity are excluded from this generalization, as the Prophet (ﷺ) said to Qubaysah bin Mukhāriq, "*O Qubaysah, asking is not permitted except in one of three cases: a man carrying responsibility for a debt [of another],[173] so he is allowed to ask until it is paid, then he should stop; and a man whose property has been destroyed by a calamity, so he is allowed to ask until he has enough to live sufficiently; and a man who has been afflicted by poverty when three rational men among his people testify to it, so he is allowed to ask until he has enough to live sufficiently. But all other requests, O Qubaysah, are unlawful gains which the solicitor consumes unlawfully.*"[174] While generosity is encouraged of wealthy believers, the poor are encouraged, whenever possible, to avoid begging and to seek Allah's approval through patience and hard work. Thus, they preserve their pride and self-respect and earn the respect of others.

---

172 See Ḥadīth No. 1.

173 This can include collecting for the purpose of paying hospital fees, blood money (diyah), or whatever is urgently needed for others, such as food, clothing, medications, etc.

174 Narrated by Aḥmad, Muslim, Abū Dāwūd and an-Nasā'i.

Hadīth No. 32

عن أبي سعد بن مالك بن سنان الخدري أن رسول الله (ﷺ) قال:

« لاَ ضَرَرَ وَلاَ ضِرَارَ»

On the authority of Abū Sa`eed, Sa`d bin Mālik bin Sinān al-Khudri, that the Messenger of Allah (ﷺ) said:

"Let there be no harm [to anyone] and no harming [in reciprocation]."

(Ḥadīth *ḥasan* narrated by Ibn Mājah, ad-Daraqutni and others and classified as *musnad*.[175] It was also related by Mālik in *al-Muwaṭṭa'* as *mursal*[176] on the authority of 'Amr bin Yaḥyā from his father from the Prophet (ﷺ) and leaving out Abū Sa'eed. It has other chains of narrators supporting one another.)

A fundamental principle presented in this ḥadīth is that harm is prohibited in every form, both to the self and to others, and that one should avoid all that is harmful. This is the basis of every *fatwā*.

Some scholars have said that the two terms "*dharar*" and "*dhirār*" are similar and mean the same. However, the Prophet (ﷺ), known for conciseness and precision in speech, is most unlikely to have used an excess word with no specific intent. In fact, grammarians have pointed to subtle differences between them:

1) "*Dharar*" is harm caused by one who benefits thereby, while "*dhirār*" is harm caused without benefit.
2) "*Dharar*" (harm) is a noun meaning damage inflicted upon something or someone initially, without his having caused harm, while "*dhirār*" (harming) is derived from a verb and means the infliction of harm in return for harm inflicted but in a different way or to a greater extent – not the restoration of justice as such, but what goes beyond it to become injustice and transgression.

Both terms suggest a violation of right.

There is no question that someone who harms another has done him injustice, and this is unlawful by authority of the Qur'ān, *sunnah* and consensus of scholars.[177] Legal retribution is another matter altogether, for in such cases the harm is done rightfully to restore justice according to Allah's law. Thus, it is clear that this ḥadīth refers to harm or injury inflicted without right, which is an obvious sin. It is not limited to those offenses listed in books of law but includes all hardship and sorrow caused to any of Allah's creatures. Examples are innumerable, but not to be overlooked are the less evident forms, such as damage to reputation and injury to feelings.

Avoiding injustice after one has been harmed is equally important, for revenge is sweet – so much so that moderation is almost impossible. How many servants of Allah have been urged on by Shayṭān into acts of excessive vengeance, thereby forfeiting any reward they would have earned and burdening themselves with sin.

---

175 A ḥadīth with a complete chain of narrators going back to the Prophet (ﷺ).
176 A ḥadīth whose chain does not include the name of a *ṣaḥābi*, wherein a *tābi'i* (successor) stated, "The Prophet (ﷺ) said..."
177 See Ḥadīth No. 24.

One who pardons and forgives is sure to gain the best of the Hereafter, yet forgiveness is not an obligation. Equity, however, is, and the balance of justice is delicate and exact. So one who fears his Lord's judgement and the possible victory of his opponent over him in the Hereafter will not meet a blow with a greater blow or an insult with a greater insult, thus tipping the balance in favor of his opponent. To avoid "*dhirār*," one who has been harmed should not himself reciprocate but rather seek amends through legal means whenever possible.

When an offender denies his offense, or part of it, and in the absence of a fair judge or an Islamic court, scholars have differed over whether or not the wrongged party has the right to take what is his by his own hand should the opportunity arise. The correct view, based upon the Prophet's ruling in the complaint of Hind about Abū Sufyān,[178] is that one may take only his right but not exceed it. This again requires a degree of honesty, *taqwā* and resolve against the promptings of Shayṭān.

---

178 Upon being told that her husband was stingy and negligent of his duty, the Prophet (ﷺ) said, "*Take from his wealth, according to what is reasonable, what is sufficient for you and your children.*" (Al-Bukhāri, Muslim, Abū Dāwūd, an-Nasā'i and Ibn Mājah)

Hadīth No. 33

عن ابن عباس أن رسول الله (ﷺ) قال:

« لَو يُعطَى النَّاسُ بِدَعوَاهُم، لادَّعَى رِجَالٌ أَموَالَ قومٍ وَدِمَاءَهُم لَكِنِ البَيِّنَةُ عَلَى المُدَّعِي، وَاليَمِينُ عَلَى مَن أَنكَرَ »

On the authority of Ibn 'Abbās that the Messenger of Allah (ﷺ) said:

"If people were given according to their claim, men would have laid claim to the properties of [another] people as well as their blood; but the [burden of] proof is on the claimant, and the oath is [incumbent] on him who denies."

(Ḥadīth *ḥasan* narrated by al-Bayhaqi and others, and part of it is found in the two *Ṣaḥeeḥs*[179])

This ḥadīth is a basic reference in cases of controversy, dispute and denial, and its ruling is applied in courts of law by the *qādhi* (legally appointed judge). The principle established is that a claim in itself is not sufficient for a right to be recognized, and unless it is accompanied by adequate proof, nothing can be awarded to a claimant. By the same measure the accused is considered innocent until proven guilty. The Prophet (ﷺ), aware of the greedy and vengeful nature of man when aided by Shayṭān, ruled decisively to limit injustice.

The burden of proof is placed upon the claimant or accuser because what is claimed is contrary to what appears as the status quo, i.e., he is stating something which, not being obvious and evident, is subject to doubt. Another precept derived from the ḥadīth is that when in doubt, it is preferable to allow a guilty party to escape penalty[180] than to risk punishing one who might be innocent. This is illustrated clearly in *Sūrah an-Nūr* where a husband who finds his wife committing adultery and swears to that is separated from her by law; however, she cannot be subject to the *hadd* punishment[181] on his word alone:

وَيَدرَؤُا عَنهَا العَذَابَ أَن تَشهَدَ أَربَعَ شَهَادَاتٍ بِاللهِ إِنَّهُ لَمِنَ الكَاذِبِينَ

"And it will prevent punishment from her that she testifies four times by Allah that he is of the liars."[182]

Likewise, the word of a dying person that "so-and-so killed me" is not sufficient in itself, but it supports other evidence submitted by the prosecution.

When proof is inadequate for conviction, an oath is taken from the accused. Such an oath is also taken from one who denies that he married, divorced, freed a slave, sold or gave his word in an agreement where possibly witnesses were not present. Before hearing the oath, the judge must warn the defendant of the gravity of his testimony and of the evil consequence in this world and the next for anyone who swears to false testimony in the name of Allah.[183]

---

179 The collections of al-Bukhāri and Muslim.

180 In this world, although he cannot escape Allah's justice in the Hereafter.

181 A punishment which is specified in the Sharī'ah, in this case, stoning until death.

182 Sūrah an-Nūr, 24:8.

183 It has been customary for the judge to warn against perjury by reciting verse 3:77 of the Qur'ān.

Once a defendant has sworn by Allah in denial of the charge, he is acquitted, but one who swears falsely to deprive another of his right is promised the wrath of Allah and Hellfire, as stated in the ḥadīth: "Whoever swears an oath which makes property due to him while he is lying will meet Allah [who is] angry with him."[184] This oath involving wealth or property is called "*al-yameen as-ṣabr,*" or the restraining oath, because it prevents the claimant from taking the right claimed by him.[185] The false oath is called "*al-yameen al-ghamūs,*" the submerging oath, because it submerges the liar deep into sin and then into Hellfire. Allah's Messenger (ﷺ) emphasized that false witnessing is among the greatest of major sins.[186]

The majority of scholars have ruled that no oath is to be taken from the claimant following that of his opponent since the ḥadīth stops short of that. In case of refusal on the part of the defendant to swear, the *qādhi* may decide, using his own judgement, but a judge can only rule according to what is apparent to him. Therefore, one who deliberately deceives him will be punished by Allah. The Prophet (ﷺ) said, "*You bring your disputes to me and perhaps one of you is more expressive in his argument than the other and I judge in his favor according to what I hear from him. So to whomever I have given something of his brother's right, I have only given a portion of the Hellfire.*"[187]

184 Narrated by al-Bukhāri and Muslim.

185 Another meaning is that the accused is restrained in custody until the oath is taken from him.

186 Al-Bukhāri.

187 Narrated by al-Bukhāri and Muslim.

Hadīth No. 34

عن أبي سعد الخدري قال: سمعت رسول الله (ﷺ) يقول:

« مَن رَأَى مِنكُم مُنكَرًا فَليُغَيِّرهُ بِيَدِهِ، فَإِن لَم يَستَطِع فَبِلِسَانِهِ، فَإِن لَم يَستَطِع فَبِقَلبِهِ، وَذَلِكَ أَضعَفُ الإِيمَانِ»

On the authority of Abū Sa'eed al-Khudri, who said: I heard the Messenger of Allah (ﷺ) say:

"Whoever of you sees a wrong – let him change it by his hand; and if he is not able, then with his tongue; and if he is not able, then with his heart – and that is the weakest of faith."

(Narrated by Muslim)

Another well-known principle of the religion has been set out by the Messenger of Allah (ﷺ) in this ḥadīth, namely, that a Muslim is required to prohibit what is wrong (*munkar*) to the extent of his ability. He will be motivated to do so not only by hope for Allah's reward and fear of His anger and punishment, but out of outrage that the merciful Creator would be forgotten or disobeyed, particularly by other Muslims, and out of concern for those who carelessly invite Allah's anger upon themselves through irresponsible acts and for society as a whole. One who earnestly seeks acceptance by Allah for himself and other believers will be conscious of this duty and not neglect it, for true brotherhood lies in assisting the other to achieve what is good and avoid what is evil in both worlds.

Its necessity lies in the fact that Allah (*subḥānahu wa ta'ālā*) has promised when corruption prevails among a people that punishments will strike not only the wicked but the righteous minority as well:

وَاتَّقُوا فِتنَةً لاَ تُصِيبَنَّ الَّذِينَ ظَلَمُوا مِنكُم خَاصَّةً وَاعلَمُوا أَنَّ اللهَ شَدِيدُ العِقَابِ

"And fear an affliction which will not strike those who have wronged among you exclusively, and know that Allah is severe in penalty."[188]

Thus, opposing *munkar* both actively and passively is a part of the faith and the way of Islam. It is not limited to those in responsible positions, for individual Muslims are knowledgeable about such matters as neglecting prayer, intoxicants, fornication, etc. As for the less obvious evils, response to these is incumbent upon the scholars who are aware of them. Failure to perform this obligation in a community leads to disastrous consequences, as Allah has warned.[189]

The Prophet's words "*whoever of you sees a wrong*" pointedly imply that the wrong (*munkar*) should be witnessed by anyone who is expected to check it. If it is known only through word of mouth and occurs in a private place, most scholars are of the opinion that one should not search, eavesdrop or enter forcibly in order to confirm a suspicion, for Allah (*subḥānahu wa ta'ālā*) has said: وَلاَ تَجَسَّسُوا ***"And do not spy."***[190] *Munkar* is to

188 Sūrah al-Anfāl, 8:25. See also 24:63.
189 See also 5:78-79.
190 Sūrah al-Ḥujurāt, 49:12.

be dealt with when discovered but not searched out.[191] Additionally, the wrong must be one determined by the standard of the *Ṣharī`ah,* one about which there is a consensus concerning its unlawfulness and not something over which scholars are in disagreement.[192]

"Let him change it" shows that the attempt to eradicate evil is an obligation; yet, there are instances when one is excused from an obligation or even prohibited from it, as the menstruating woman is from *ṣalāh.* This obligation also carries with it certain conditions and regulations. Moreover, it is a collective obligation (*fardh kifayāh*)[193] and might be incumbent upon specific persons but not others, such as the ones actually aware of a problem or an individual who is the only one capable of putting it to an end.

Allah's Messenger (ﷺ) mentioned three ways to oppose *munkar*:

1) By the hand, i.e., physical means

This is for those who are able to deal with the problem directly and are likely to be in a position of authority, such as the head of state or the head of a family, whose order is normally obeyed. His duty is not only to command cessation but to enforce it as far as possible. Changing by the hand might include the destruction of what is instrumental to the *munkar,* such as the containers of intoxicants, subversive literature, a house of prostitution, etc.

It has been noted that the most extreme of such measures is *jihad* in Allah's cause and the carrying out of legal punishments against convicted criminals. Enforcement of the entire *Sharī`ah* law is the responsibility of any head of state. Al-Imām Aḥmad emphasized, however, that arms should not be taken up against oppressive Muslim rulers due to several prophetic ḥadīths urging patience in the face of such trials and to the fear that such action might lead to greater evils, namely civil strife and extensive bloodshed among Muslims. Physical prevention of *munkar* committed by rulers is restricted to preventing their acts of injustice and destroying their unlawful possessions if it is possible. In any event, physical force, when feared to cause greater conflict or damaging consequences, is no longer permissible.

2) By the tongue

This method is used by those who either do not have direct access to abolish the evil themselves or have witnessed what cannot be changed by the hand, such as deception, backbiting or adherence to innovations in religious matters, or by those who occupy subordinate positions. Such persons can only warn or advise the offending party or the public at large concerning the evil which is apparent to them in hope that it will be stopped. The guidance of wrongdoers is an obligation upon all knowledgeable believers. Once a person (or group) has performed this duty, he is not then accountable if the offender does not comply, since the removal of *munkar* will depend upon other than himself.

---

191 Exceptions have been cited for cases of urgency, e.g., when it is reported that someone is about to be murdered, assaulted, robbed, etc. at a certain location. Aggressive measures can be taken to prevent an expected crime.

192 i.e., a variance of viewpoints based upon evidence from the Qur'ān or sunnah, not merely personal or sectarian positions, which are not to be considered.

193 Meaning that when a sufficient number of qualified people perform the duty, the rest are exempted.

It is thus imperative that utmost perception and diplomacy be used on such occasions in an attempt to avoid angry reactions and obstinacy on the part of those being warned.[194] Al-Imām ash-Shāfi'i said, "He who admonishes his brother privately has advised him and honored him, but he who admonishes him publicly has exposed him and shamed him." Besides a gentle manner which shows concern for the wrongdoer,[195] one must be convincing, which requires knowledge of the rulings derived from the Qur'ān and sunnah, skill in expression, as well as insight into the motivations of men. This is what comprises ability. Verbal opposition to *munkar* may be addressed to specific persons who commit wrongs or it might be general, in the form of *da`wah* to non-Muslims, advice given in a lecture, or a Friday sermon.

Fear of insult or disdain by evildoers will not absolve the qualified person from this duty, contrary to the threat of bodily harm. No Muslim is under obligation to endure torture or unjust imprisonment. The Prophet's statement that the best *jihād* is a word of truth before a tyrannical ruler,[196] with knowledge that the speaker exposes himself to danger and possibly death, is an indication by him (ﷺ) of what is meritorious and not what is obligatory. Several scholars have added that one who is certain his advice will not be accepted, due to the hostility of the evildoers or their lack of respect for him generally, is also exempted from the obligation.[197]

The two aforementioned methods of combating *munkar* are binding upon those with the ability to effect change. Inability is related to lack of knowledge or lack of proficiency, physical limitations, and the expectation of harmful repercussions. The same efforts become forbidden when they could lead to greater evils.

3) In the heart

This is an obligation upon every Muslim without exception, for even if one is unable to change an evil by means of his hand or his tongue, he cannot accept it in his heart and remain a believer. This is evident from the Prophet's words, "*and that is the weakest of faith*," meaning that without objection and disapproval in the heart, faith does not remain. Al-Imām an-Nawawi explained that this does not mean a person who opposes wrongdoing in his heart because he is unable to effect a change by other means is weaker in faith than another. It merely means that the least one can do in such a situation is to bear it unwillingly with the conviction that were it possible for him to stop it in some way, he would do so, and that this kind of faith is weakest only because it does not, in fact, alter the status quo, so it is weakest in effect. And Allah knows best.

---

194 The exception is toward one who proudly flaunts his sin before the people. Such a shameless one is deserving of harsher treatment.

195 Note Allah's instruction to Musa on how to approach the tyrant, Fir`aun (20:44 and 79:17-19).

196 In a ḥadīth narrated by Aḥmad and Ibn Mājah – *ṣaḥeeḥ*.

197 Some others, however, disagree, quoting verse 164 of Sūrah al-A'rāf and pointing out that the duty is to remind and advise, absolving oneself before Allah, and not to ensure acceptance of the advice.

Hadīth No. 35

عن أبي هريرة قال: قال رسول الله (ﷺ):

«لاَ تَحَاسَدُوا، وَلاَ تَنَاجَشُوا، وَلاَ تَبَاغَضُوا، وَلاَ تَدَابَرُوا، وَلاَ يَبِعْ بَعضُكُم عَلَى بَيعِ بَعضٍ، وَكُونُوا عِبَادَ اللهِ إِخوَانًا المُسلِمُ أَخُو المُسلِمِ: لاَ يَظلِمُهُ، وَلاَ يَخذُلُهُ، وَلاَ يَكذِبُهُ، وَلاَ يَحقِرُهُ. التَّقوَى هٰهُنَا – وَيُشِيرُ إِلَى صَدرِهِ ثَلاَثَ مَرَّاتٍ – بِحَسبِ امرِئٍ مِنَ الشَّرِّ أَن يَحقِرَ أَخَاهُ المُسلِمَ. كُلُّ المُسلِمِ عَلَى المُسلِمِ حَرَامٌ: دَمُهُ، وَمَالُهُ، وَعِرضُهُ»

On the authority of Abū Hurayrah, who said: The Messenger of Allah (ﷺ) said:

"Do not envy one another; do not deceive one another in bidding; do not hate one another; do not turn your backs on one another; and do not intrude on the transactions of one another, but be, O servants of Allah, brothers. A Muslim is the brother of a Muslim: he neither oppresses him nor abandons him; he neither lies to him nor looks down on him. Righteousness is right here – and he pointed to his breast three times. It is sufficient evil for a person to look down upon his brother Muslim. The whole of a Muslim to another Muslim is inviolable: his blood, his property and his honor."

(Narrated by Muslim)

The Prophet (ﷺ) repeatedly confirmed that Islam is not limited to a declaration of belief and particular rites of worship, but it includes morals and manners. True consciousness of Allah and fear of Him is evident in the way one deals with others. Islam encourages the perfection of moral character and condemns hypocrisy. Brotherhood is not simply an ideal or a slogan proclaimed, but rather it is a moral commitment whose practice was taught actively by the Messenger of Allah (ﷺ). Respect and consideration for others is the basis of brotherhood. In this ḥadīth the Prophet (ﷺ) prohibits certain actions which prevent its realization, among them:

Envy – More specifically, the desire that a blessing bestowed upon another would be removed from him. It is prohibited because it is harmful to the envier, causing him distress without benefit and perhaps leading him to sinful speech or actions that harm his soul in the Hereafter. It is also an expression of dissatisfaction with what Allah has willed and rebellion against Him, especially when accompanied by efforts to change the good condition of the one envied. Such an attitude can only earn Allah's anger; therefore, natural inclinations toward selfishness must be disciplined and regulated.

Envious people are of different kinds:

1. One who seeks to remove a blessing from another and transfer it to himself. This is prohibited and blameworthy.

2. One who seeks to remove a blessing from another without wishing it for himself. He is more evil than the first.

3. One who has feelings of envy within himself but does not act upon them directly, and these are of two categories:

   a. One overcome by feeling in spite of himself and unable to rid himself of it. Such a person is not considered sinful.

b. One who allows himself to envy and dwells upon it rather than occupying himself with other matters. Such a person can hardly avoid sinful speech. He is often found striving to obtain the same worldly benefits as the one he envies, but this in itself is not prohibited when the other is not adversely affected by it. On the other hand, when envy concerns religious matters and is manifested by competitiveness in performing virtuous deeds and seeking greater reward in the Hereafter, it becomes a merit as illustrated by the Prophet (ﷺ) in several ḥadīths related to intention.

4. One who, upon finding envy within himself, strives to do away with it and replace it with happiness at the good fortune of his brother, love for him, and pride in his accomplishment. This is the true believer who likes for his brother what he likes for himself.[198]

Deception of a buyer by offering a higher price for something on sale without the intention of buying – Thus, the potential buyer is forced to pay a higher price than he would have done otherwise. The literal meaning of "*najsh*" is "bait," i.e., that which is offered by a hunter to lure a prey. Such action is prohibited whether done in conspiracy with the seller or separately, merely to harm a buyer by making him pay more unnecessarily.

It is also correct to interpret it in a wider sense which would include all methods of dealing with others through deception and scheming, particularly in trade, by adding unwanted goods to a sale, raising prices through false claims, concealing faults in merchandise, or any other form of cheating.

Hating one another – Scholars have noted that it is not always possible to control feelings and that dislike can creep into the heart without one's intending it. Therefore, the words "Do not hate one another" are interpreted to mean: do not practice anything which causes hate or aggravates it. To this end the Messenger of Allah (ﷺ) warned sternly against gossip and backbiting, a major sin in Islam, and permitted the lie which is spoken for the purpose of restoring good relations between people. At the same time, every Muslim should be careful not to hate another merely out of custom or because of a personal whim.

Not included in this prohibition is the hatred of Allah's enemies, which is an essential part of the faith. But al-Imām Ibn Rajab pointed out that when people began to differ over religion and separate into factions, hatred grew among them. Each of them claimed that his hatred was in the cause of Allah. Yet, some were justified and others were not, for they may have been swayed by personal passions and loyalties, customary prejudices and the like. So a believer must always be acutely aware of his motivations and check himself honestly in this regard.

Turning one's back on another, i.e., boycotting him or becoming an enemy to him – It is unlawful to sever relations with another Muslim over worldly differences or personal grievances, as confirmed in the ḥadīth narrated by al-Bukhāri, Muslim and others: "*It is not permissible for a Muslim to shun his brother for over three nights while they meet and each avoids the other. The best of them is the one who begins with*

---

198 Refer to Ḥadīth No. 13.

greeting." Al-Imām Aḥmad added that the greeting should be accompanied by sincere affection and not merely words which could be uttered in a tone of animosity. Other scholars have offered that in the case of relatives the right is greater, so greeting alone is insufficient and the relationship must return to the state it enjoyed before the alienation.

However, when the boycott is for religious reasons or for discipline, such as the refusal to associate with consumers of intoxicants, slanderers or others who commit major sins, it may last longer than three days. This is evidenced by the incident of the three who excused themselves from the Tabūk expedition, when the Prophet (ﷺ) ordered a boycott of them which continued for fifty days until Allah revealed that He had accepted their repentance. Disciplinary measures of this sort may be taken when necessary, for it is well known that the Prophet (ﷺ) kept away from his wives for a month on one occasion.

Intrusion on a transaction – What is meant is the entrance of a third party with a better offer after an agreement has been reached between two sides over a sale, particularly concerning the price. This practice has been prohibited in numerous other ḥadīth*s* due to the harm caused to social relations. Several of these ḥadīth*s* also include the prohibition of seeking a woman in marriage whose family has been approached by another suitor until she has refused him. In the absence of an agreement the third party may make an offer.

The Messenger of Allah (ﷺ) then ordered all believers to be brothers, as if to say that by refraining from the prohibited acts and being conscious of the rights of others brotherhood will develop naturally. He went on to state that a brother is to be respected and spared bad treatment of every kind, giving the following examples:

Oppression and injustice, i.e., harming another in regard to his person, his religion, his property or his honor without legal right – Allah (*subḥānahu wa ta'ālā*) prohibited injustice from Himself and then from His servants.[199]

Abandoning one in need – The believer is expected to help and support his brother in the lawful affairs of worldly life and in religion. When the Prophet (ﷺ) said to his companions, "*Help your brother whether oppressed or an oppressor,*" they inquired as to how one should help an oppressor. He (ﷺ) replied, "*By preventing him from oppression.*"[200]

Lying – It is the right of every person to be told the truth. Lying to a Muslim for any purpose other than bringing about reconciliation or protecting him is cheating and betrayal.

Considering another Muslim inferior – Looking down upon another means considering oneself better than him in some way. That was the sin of Iblees when he refused to bow in respect to Adam, saying:

قَالَ أَنَا خَيرٌ مِنهُ خَلَقتَنِي مِن نَارٍ وَخَلَقتَهُ مِن طِينٍ

"I am better than him. You created me from fire and created him from clay."[201]

---

199 See Ḥadīth No. 24.
200 Narrated by al-Bukhāri and Muslim.
201 Sūrah al-A'rāf, 7:12.

This attitude is sinful because it contradicts that of Allah (*subḥānahu wa ta'ālā*), who did not hold any man in contempt when He created him. Rather, He created him in the best upright form, honored him, sent him guidance, and made him a responsible being. Allah (*subḥānahu wa ta'ālā*) considered him worth creating and sustaining, and He alone is able to judge him perfectly. Therefore, no one should judge another by his worldly appearance, for perhaps a humble servant is more noble in the sight of Allah than one of position among the people. The true believer, well aware of his own faults, will assume that others have more goodness in them or less sins than himself, and in fact, no one knows how another will end up in the Hereafter, for the Day of Judgement is described by Allah as خَافِضَةٌ رَّافِعَةٌ ***"that which brings down [some] and elevates [others]."***[202] In his commentary al-Imām an-Nawawi stated that one should not even assume that a non-believer is from the people of Hell because it is possible that he might embrace Islam before his death.

Valid criticism, however, such as criticism of wickedness or ignorance, is directed at those traits in particular individuals and not their persons. It is not included here since it does not detract from their standing as human beings with specific rights. Gossiping about them, however, is forbidden. Looking down upon others is caused by pride, conceit and arrogance, and these are among the greatest evils which prevent one from entering Paradise. The Messenger (ﷺ) warned, "*No one will enter Paradise who has in his heart an atom's weight of pride.*" When questioned about pride, he elucidated, "*Pride is disregarding rights and looking down upon people.*"[203] And he (ﷺ) said, "*Shall I not inform you about the people of Paradise? Every weak, oppressed person who, if he swore that Allah would do something, He would do it for him.*[204] *Shall I not inform you about the people of Hellfire? Every cruel, arrogant oppressor.*"[205] Hence, the Prophet (ﷺ) concluded, "*It is sufficient evil for a person to look down upon his brother Muslim,*" meaning that it is sufficient to make him enter Hell.

By emphasizing that *taqwā*[206] is in the heart, he (ﷺ) again alluded to the fact that one cannot judge another by appearance or even by his deeds. For righteousness is an inner virtue, the extent of which is known only to Allah, who said:

إِنَّ أَكرَمَكُم عِندَ اللهِ أَتقَاكُم

> ***"Indeed, the most noble of you in the sight of Allah is the most righteous."***[207]

In conclusion, the Prophet (ﷺ) restated the inviolability of every Muslim – his person, property and honor. This statement was made repeatedly by him on occasions where people were gathered, most notably during the farewell pilgrimage on the day of 'Arafah, the day of sacrifice, and the second day of *tashreeq* in Mina. Every kind of abuse without right has been prohibited, even to the degree of frightening people or annoying them. Allah (*subḥānahu wa ta'ālā*) has said:

---

202 Sūrah al-Wāqi'ah, 56:3.
203 Narrated by Muslim.
204 Because of his high position in the sight of Allah, meaning one who is a sincere believer.
205 Narrated by al-Bukhāri, Muslim and Aḥmad.
206 Righteousness, piety, fear of Allah.
207 Sūrah al-Ḥujurāt, 49:13.

وَالَّذِينَ يُؤْذُونَ الْمُؤْمِنِينَ وَالْمُؤْمِنَاتِ بِغَيْرِ مَا اكْتَسَبُوا فَقَدِ احْتَمَلُوا بُهْتَانًا وَإِثْمًا مُبِينًا

"And those who harm believing men and believing women for other than what they have earned have taken upon themselves a falsehood and manifest sin."[208]

And a severe warning was issued by the Prophet (ﷺ) to those who violate the sanctity of brotherhood: *"Do not harm the servants of Allah, do not revile them, and do not pursue their faults. For one who pursues the fault of his brother Muslim – Allah will pursue his fault until He exposes him [even] inside his house."*[209]

Ḥadīth No. 36

عن أبي هريرة عن النبي (ﷺ) قال:

«مَنْ نَفَّسَ عَنْ مُؤْمِنٍ كُرْبَةً مِنْ كُرَبِ الدُّنْيَا نَفَّسَ اللهُ عَنْهُ كُرْبَةً مِنْ كُرَبِ يَوْمِ الْقِيَامَةِ. وَمَنْ يَسَّرَ عَلَى مُعْسِرٍ، يَسَّرَ اللهُ عَلَيْهِ فِي الدُّنْيَا وَالآخِرَةِ. وَمَنْ سَتَرَ مُسْلِمًا سَتَرَهُ اللهُ فِي الدُّنْيَا وَالآخِرَةِ. وَاللهُ فِي عَوْنِ الْعَبْدِ مَا كَانَ الْعَبْدُ فِي عَوْنِ أَخِيهِ. وَمَنْ سَلَكَ طَرِيقًا يَلْتَمِسُ فِيهِ عِلْمًا سَهَّلَ اللهُ لَهُ بِهِ طَرِيقًا إِلَى الْجَنَّةِ. وَمَا اجْتَمَعَ قَوْمٌ فِي بَيْتٍ مِنْ بُيُوتِ اللهِ، يَتْلُونَ كِتَابَ اللهِ وَيَتَدَارَسُونَهُ بَيْنَهُمْ، إِلاَّ نَزَلَتْ عَلَيْهِمُ السَّكِينَةُ، وَغَشِيَتْهُمُ الرَّحْمَةُ، وَحَفَّتْهُمُ الْمَلَائِكَةُ، وَذَكَرَهُمُ اللهُ فِيمَنْ عِنْدَهُ، وَمَنْ بَطَّأَ بِهِ عَمَلُهُ لَمْ يُسْرِعْ بِهِ نَسَبُهُ»

On the authority of Abū Hurayrah that the Prophet (ﷺ) said:

"Whoever relieves a believer of a distress from the distresses of this world – Allah will relieve him of a distress from the distresses of the Day of Resurrection. And whoever facilitates [a matter] for one in financial difficulty – Allah will facilitate for him [matters] in this world and the Hereafter. And whoever covers [the fault of] a Muslim – Allah will cover his [faults] in this world and the Hereafter. Allah is in aid of [His] servant as long as the servant is in aid of his brother. And whoever follows a path seeking knowledge therein – Allah will facilitate for him a path to Paradise. No people assemble in one of the houses of Allah reciting the Book of Allah and studying it among themselves but that tranquility descends upon them, mercy envelops them, the angels surround them, and Allah mentions them among those with Him. And he whose deeds slow him down will not be accelerated by his lineage."

(Narrated by Muslim in these words)

The ḥadīth begins with a continuation of the theme of brotherhood and Muslims' duties toward one another. While the previous one contained a prohibition of every kind of harm and abuse, this ḥadīth encourages aid, support and protection by showing the resulting rewards and benefits. The good tidings included therein motivate a

---

208 Sūrah al-Aḥzāb, 33:58.
209 Narrated by Aḥmad – ḥasan.

believer to serve people and to join those who seek knowledge and study the Qur'ān.

Additionally, the ḥadīth is among those which illustrate that a reward or punishment is often related in kind to the deed itself. For when a Muslim saves another from oppression, injustice, captivity, debt, fear, hunger, poverty, slander, injury or any difficulty he might face in life, Allah, in turn, will save him from one of the difficulties of the Hereafter, which is infinitely greater than any of this world. Thus, the reward is of the same type, although many times greater than the original deed, its extent being known only to Allah. If one contemplates the terrors of the resurrection, the anguish of awaiting judgement with knowledge of his sins, and the desperate need of each soul for any good deed at that time, he will perceive the state of a believer who, in the midst of that grave situation, is overtaken by Allah's justice and mercy and rewarded for every instance in which he aided or worked to alleviate the affliction of one of his brothers during his life on earth.

Al-Imām an-Nawawi added, "Within the ḥadīth is another secret which appears through deduction: a promise by the Truthful (ﷺ) that a Muslim who relieves another of distress will have a good end and die within Islam because a disbeliever cannot receive mercy in the Hereafter and nothing will relieve his distress." The *Imām* thus concluded that relieving a believer of distress is the most excellent of deeds (following the religious obligations).

Undoubtedly, the greatest distress on the Day of Resurrection is fear of entering Hellfire. Several authentic ḥadīths relate that Allah (*subḥānahu wa ta'ālā*) forgave a certain servant because of some deed of mercy done by him – even so much as drawing water for a thirsty dog. On more than one occasion the Prophet (ﷺ) cited the alleviation of debt for a destitute person as a cause for Allah's overlooking the benefactor's own shortcomings and forgiving his sins, thus saving him from Hell. This may be done by granting additional time for payments, waiving part or all of a debt, or by paying part or all of a debt owed to another.

As for covering the fault of a Muslim, several other ḥadīths express this concept, among them narrations which threaten exposure of those who seek out and disclose the faults of others, as in that of Aḥmad previously cited.[210] One early scholar observed, "I came upon a people without apparent faults, but when they mentioned the faults of others, the people mentioned their faults..." Had they refrained, their own defects would not have become known, but by transgressing they invited retaliation. This pattern is easily perceived in worldly life, but the Prophet (ﷺ) made it clear that the offenders will be disgraced in the Hereafter as well. On the contrary, a Muslim who conceals the imperfections in his brother will be treated in a like manner by Allah (*subḥānahu wa ta'ālā*) at the time of Judgement.

What is intended, obviously, is concealment of the deficiencies, errors, weaknesses and failures of those Muslims who generally appear to be upright and honorable but might fall into sin occasionally. The reputations of ordinary Muslims are to be protected, and indeed, seeking out or mentioning their faults is a sign of hypocrisy and disregard for the well-being of the community. This does not mean, however, that one

---

210 Concluding the commentary on Ḥadīth No. 35.

should not prevent them from wrongdoing, advise them or help them to overcome their shortcomings, for that is a duty as well,[211] but it must be done without alerting others as far as possible. Also to be concealed are sins of the past for which a Muslim has repented and reformed himself. Unnecessary reference to his previous behavior is an act of aggression and injury for which Allah will surely avenge him. Similarly, a Muslim should not speak of sins he himself has committed unless to seek a *fatwa* or for legal testimony. Instead, he must repent sincerely and privately to Allah. Then Allah will conceal his sin and forgive him for it on the Day of Judgement.

Such restraint does not apply in the case of those who commit sins openly and shamelessly without regard to society or fear of Allah. Nor does it apply for known criminals who threaten security. These must not be shielded, for it will only encourage them to increase their evil activities and spread corruption in the land. Exposure of them and warning against them is not seen as backbiting but is a social obligation. Beyond that, it could even be necessary to report them to the state authority.

In addition, it is permissible and sometimes imperative to offer public advice or criticism to those in positions of responsibility if they do not respond to private counsel. The sunnah of the Prophet's rightly guided successors established this as, for example, when Abū Bakr said, "Support me as long as I do well, and if I err, set me straight." And 'Umar announced upon assuming the caliphate, "Let anyone who sees in me a deviation straighten it." The principle is not limited to rulers and governors but applies to every carrier of a trust.[212] It is not permissible to keep silent when qualifications are in question or when injustice may be done. Criticism of methods or conclusions by scholars of one another is valid as long as it remains within the limits of objectivity and righteous intention.

The Messenger of Allah (ﷺ) did not specify any particular kind of aid that could be given to a Muslim brother, meaning that the statement is general and comprehensive. So any assistance a servant is able to offer from his wealth, physical ability or influence is sufficient to earn him the aid of Allah in his own affairs. Conversely, the Prophet (ﷺ) warned, "*Whoever does not show mercy to people – Allah will not show mercy to him.*"[213]

No society will be strong and productive unless it is built upon the principle of cooperation, just as mutual trust and concern produces positive responses in its individual members. Allah's Messenger (ﷺ) was the most perfect example of all that he taught, and there are countless and varied examples of such behavior among his companions and their students. The concept is defined and qualified by Allah (*subḥānahu wa ta'ālā*) in His injunction:

وَتَعَاوَنُوا عَلَى الْبِرِّ وَالتَّقْوَى وَلاَ تَعَاوَنُوا عَلَى الإِثْمِ وَالْعُدْوَانِ

> ***"And cooperate in righteousness and piety but do not cooperate in sin and aggression."***[214]

The Prophet (ﷺ) then brought attention to another type of deed, although it is not

211 Refer to Ḥadīth No. 34 and No. 35.

212 Such as a narrator of ḥadīth, a court witness, a guardian of orphans or property, etc.

213 Narrated by Aḥmad, Muslim and al-Bukhāri.

214 Sūrah al-Ma'idah, 5:2.

unrelated to the aforementioned. The Muslim has been encouraged, even ordered, to seek knowledge and promised that this will lead him to Paradise. What is intended primarily is religious knowledge, although worldly knowledge employed for a good and lawful purpose cannot be excluded. Again, this obligation is both personal (*fardh `ayn*) and collective (*fardh kifāyah*). For every Muslim, male and female, is charged with obtaining sufficient knowledge to worship correctly and manage his daily affairs, while the community is charged with producing a sufficient number of religious scholars. Both religious and secular knowledge are subject to certain stipulations in order to make it acceptable to Allah and that for which He will facilitate a path to Paradise:

1) It must be pursued seeking the acceptance of Allah.
2) Once obtained, it must be acted upon in the way ordained by Allah.
3) It must be shared and spread among the people.
4) It must not be used for showing off or solely for worldly benefits, for knowledge is of two kinds: that on the tongue, which is Allah's evidence against a servant; and that in the heart, which is beneficial knowledge, making a person righteous and effective.
5) One must be honest about his own limitations, admitting when he does not know something about which he is asked. As it has been said: "I do not know" is half of knowledge.

When he spoke of people assembling for recitation and study of the Qur'ān, the Prophet (ﷺ) did not specify that they be learned or pious or those of particular qualities or positions; any group gathering for this purpose with sincere intention can reap the four benefits mentioned by him (ﷺ). Houses of Allah are normally understood to be mosques. However, some scholars have interpreted the meaning here to be any place where Muslims meet, including homes, particularly in the case of women, whose worship at home is preferable to that in a mosque.

In conclusion, Allah's Messenger (ﷺ) reminds His servants that it is only righteous deeds which help one along on his way to Paradise and raise him to its highest positions. As stated in the Qur'ān:

وَلِكُلٍّ دَرَجَاتٌ مِمَّا عَمِلُوا

"And for all are degrees [resulting] from what they did."[215]

Hastening to good deeds during one's lifetime on earth will hasten his entrance into Paradise on the Day of Judgement when, as the Prophet (ﷺ) described,[216] a narrow bridge will be placed over the raging pit of Hellfire upon which every servant must pass. The disbelievers and unrepentant will fail in crossing and be pulled into the Fire. The believers will cross according to their deeds, some at the speed of lightning, others at the speed of the wind, others at the speed of horses, some running, some walking, some crawling on their knees, terrified and barely escaping. When they have crossed they will enter Paradise, the speed and ease of that determined by their deeds.

---

215 Sūrah al-An`ām, 6:132.

216 In ḥadīths narrated by al-Bukhārī and Muslim.

By stating that أَكْرَمَكُمْ عِنْدَ اللهِ أَتْقَاكُمْ *"the most noble of you is the most righteous,"*[217] Allah (subḥānahu wa ta'ālā) put an end to pre-Islamic standards of evaluation: wealth, class and lineage. The tribe and family were of particular importance to the Arabs, but even the Prophet (ﷺ), while warning his closest kinsmen, declared that he had no power to benefit any of them before Allah, stating, "O family of Bani Hāshim, O family of `Abdul-Muṭṭalib, O Fāṭimah daughter of Muḥammad, save yourselves from the Fire."[218] Thus, he confirmed that all men are born with equal status in the sight of Allah and that each must prove his true worth during his stay upon the earth. So any who think they can depend upon social status or worldly influence to serve their interests in the Hereafter are gravely mistaken.[219]

Ḥadīth No. 37

عن ابن عباس عن رسول الله (ﷺ) فيما يرويه عن ربه تبارك وتعالى قال:

« إِنَّ اللهَ كَتَبَ الْحَسَنَاتِ وَالسَّيِّئَاتِ، ثُمَّ بَيَّنَ ذَلِكَ: فَمَنْ هَمَّ بِحَسَنَةٍ فَلَمْ يَعْمَلْهَا كَتَبَهَا اللهُ عِنْدَهُ حَسَنَةً كَامِلَةً، وَإِنْ هَمَّ بِهَا فَعَمِلَهَا كَتَبَهَا اللهُ عِنْدَهُ عَشْرَ حَسَنَاتٍ إِلَى سَبْعِمِائَةِ ضِعْفٍ إِلَى أَضْعَافٍ كَثِيرَةٍ، وَإِنْ هَمَّ بِسَيِّئَةٍ فَلَمْ يَعْمَلْهَا كَتَبَهَا اللهُ عِنْدَهُ حَسَنَةً كَامِلَةً، وَإِنْ هَمَّ بِهَا فَعَمِلَهَا كَتَبَهَا اللهُ سَيِّئَةً وَاحِدَةً»

On the authority of Ibn 'Abbās from the Messenger of Allah (ﷺ) is that among the sayings he relates from his Lord (glorified and exalted be He) is that He said:

"Allah has registered the good deeds and the bad ones. Then He clarified it, [saying], 'He who intended [to do] a good deed and did not do it – Allah writes it with Himself as a complete good deed; and if he intended it and did it – Allah writes it with Himself as ten good deeds up to seven hundred times or many times [over that]. And if he intended [to do] a bad deed and did not do it – Allah writes it with Himself as a complete good deed; but if he intended it and did it – Allah writes it as one bad deed.'"

(Narrated by al-Bukhāri and Muslim in their two Ṣaḥeeḥs in these words)

Perhaps no ḥadīth in this collection is more inclusive of all the believer's life than this one, which covers each of his deeds and intentions. Its meaning is expressed in many authentic narrations from the Prophet (ﷺ) and shows the generosity of Allah (subḥānahu wa ta'ālā) and His favor to His creation.

The ḥadīth contains four categories:

1) **The good deed** – Its minimum reward is that of ten deeds[220] because the servant was not content with desire alone but exerted effort to accomplish the deed as well. A reward in excess of ten times is given according to Allah's knowledge of His servant's

---

217 Sūrah al-Ḥujurāt, 49:13.
218 Narrated by Aḥmad and Muslim.
219 For Qur'ānic evidences refer to 23:101-103, 31:33, 66:10, 69:28-29, 70:11-15 and 80:33-37.
220 For Qur'ānic evidence see Sūrah al-An'ām, 6:160.

righteousness, the sincerity of his intention, the type of deed done, the effort expended, and its suitability to the situation at hand.

The Qur'ān mentions spending for the cause of Allah as a deed which earns the reward of 700 times or more:

مَثَلُ الَّذِينَ يُنفِقُونَ أَمْوَالَهُم فِي سَبِيلِ اللَّهِ كَمَثَلِ حَبَّةٍ أَنبَتَتْ سَبْعَ سَنَابِلَ فِي كُلِّ سُنبُلَةٍ مِائَةُ حَبَّةٍ وَاللَّهُ يُضَاعِفُ لِمَن يَشَاءُ وَاللَّهُ وَاسِعٌ عَلِيمٌ

"The example of those who spend their wealth in the way of Allah is like a seed [of grain] which grows seven spikes; in each spike is a hundred grains; and Allah multiplies [that] for whom He wills. And Allah is all-Encompassing and Knowing."[221]

And when a man gave a she-camel in charity, the Prophet (ﷺ) said, "*You will have for her on the Day of Resurrection 700 she-camels.*"[222]

A deed begun earns a multiple reward even though the servant might be prevented from its completion or might not find the good result he had expected when performing it. This is because Allah (subḥānahu wa ta`ālā) rewards according to the best results a deed could possibly have produced – as if a man gave a *dirham* to a needy person who bought something with it and sold it at the highest profit, from which he gave charity and bought again; then he sold at the highest profit, this process being repeated year after year. Or as if someone planted a seed with a sincere intention and it grew in the most fertile ground under the best conditions, thereby producing the greatest number of seeds which grew and reproduced in the same way until the Day of Resurrection. Or as if a word of knowledge or advice was spoken and heard by the largest number of people, who benefited and passed it on to the largest number of people generation after generation until the Day of Resurrection, and so on. Thus, the deed is multiplied in the evaluation of Allah until its reward reaches 700 times or beyond, but Allah knows best.

When mentioning a reward "many times" in excess of 700, the Prophet (ﷺ) cited no limit. Indeed, Allah Himself stated in the Qur'ān:

إِنَّمَا يُوَفَّى الصَّابِرُونَ أَجْرَهُم بِغَيْرِ حِسَابٍ

"Those who are patient will be given their reward without account,"[223]

because patience in the face of what one dislikes is among the most difficult of deeds. In a ḥadīth qudsi He (subḥānahu wa ta`ālā) declared, "*Fasting is Mine and I reward for it,*"[224] without indication of the extent of that reward, perhaps since fasting is a deed of patience. These unlimited multiples are known only to Allah, who grants them in generous appreciation of even the smallest deeds.

2) **The bad deed** – Once committed, it is registered as a single deed with no addition.

---

221 Sūrah al-Baqarah, 2:261.
222 Narrated by Muslim.
223 Sūrah az-Zumar, 39:10.
224 Al-Bukhāri, Muslim and others. A ḥadīth qudsi is a revelation from Allah recounted in the words of the Prophet (ﷺ).

Due to Allah's perfect justice, punishment will not exceed the limit of that one deed, its extent and proportion being known precisely by Him. However, all scholars agree, based upon evidences from the Qur'ān and sunnah, that a wrongdoing becomes greater and more sinful in certain places, particularly the Ḥaram in Makkah, and at certain times, such as during the four sacred months[225] and in Ramadhān. Therefore, its punishment is increased accordingly. In addition, an evil deed is worse when done by a person of nobility and knowledge, and most especially one in a position of leadership and responsibility. The Qur'ān confirmed this when it stated that had the Prophet (ﷺ) or any of his wives deviated or sinned, they would have been punished by Allah more severely than an ordinary person.[226]

When a bad deed has been registered, it may yet be erased through true repentance,[227] as suggested in the ḥadīth: "*The repentant is as one without sin.*"[228] When Allah forgives His servant, the deed is removed from his record. One particular aspect of repentance, the performance of additional good deeds seeking the acceptance of Allah and amendment of one's relationship with Him, serves this purpose as well:

إِنَّ الْحَسَنَاتِ يُذْهِبْنَ السَّيِّئَاتِ

"Indeed, good deeds do away with bad deeds." [229]

3) **The intent to do a good deed** – The meaning of the word "*hamma*" (planned or intended) falls somewhere between that of desire and determination. It is the process of mentally preparing oneself to carry out a particular action, an inclination which would likely be acted upon when circumstances favor it and not merely a thought which crosses the mind.

Allah (*subḥānahu wa ta'ālā*) considers this intent as a good deed and registers it as such because it is, in fact, the initiation of a deed and the first step toward its accomplishment. So even when hindered by unfavorable circumstances or prevented by some obstacle, the believer's righteous inclination is appreciated by Allah, who rewards it according to His complete knowledge of that servant.[230] Then, when the deed is undertaken, that reward is multiplied.

Several narrations cite specific examples of reward for intent, like that about one who plans to awaken for prayer at night but is overcome by sleep until the morning or one who wishes for wealth so that he could spend it in the way of Allah. The earnest desire for an opportunity to prove oneself to Allah is sufficient to earn His favor. As the Prophet (ﷺ) reported, "*Whoever asks [Allah] to be killed in Allah's cause, truthfully from his heart, will be given by Allah the reward of a martyr even though he might die upon his bed.*"[231] Thus, early scholars used to advise someone who wanted to work continually

---

225 i.e., Dhul-Qa'dah, Dhul-Ḥijjah, Muḥarram and Rajab.

226 See Sūrah al-Israa', 17:73-75 and Sūrah al-Aḥzāb, 33:30.

227 For the requirements of acceptable repentance, refer to the commentary of Ḥadīth No. 18.

228 Narrated by Ibn Mājah – ḥasan.

229 Sūrah Hūd, 11:114.

230 This ḥadīth disproves the popular English saying, "Hell is paved with good intentions." Allah (*subḥānahu wa ta`ālā*) extends every mercy to His believing servants.

231 Aḥmad, Abū Dāwūd, Ibn Mājah and others – ṣaḥeeḥ.

for Allah, "Do good as long as you are able, and when you slacken or cease, have the intent to do it [when you can]." Thus, good deeds are always being recorded.

4) **The intent to do a bad deed** – An evil intent is not recorded until it is translated into effort.[232] Then it is either carried out, and thus registered, or consciously eliminated through self-restraint. The prevention of evil being a virtue, Allah considers refraining or preventing oneself from it as a good deed, in fact, a complete good deed, registered and rewarded as such. It should be remembered, however, that in other narrations of al-Bukhāri and Muslim there is a stipulation by Allah (*subḥānahu wa taʿālā*) "that he [i.e., the servant] abandoned it only for Me." So restraint becomes a good deed when it results from the remembrance of Allah – fear of His anger and desire for His approval. But if one should decide against an intended bad deed for fear of people or of their blame, or if he is prevented from it by external obstacles, or if he gives it up due to loss of desire or physical inability, it will not be rewarded by Allah because the proper intention is lacking for that deed, rendering it invalid.

In conclusion, a few points remain to be mentioned:

- The generous favor described in this ḥadīth is obtained only by believers since deeds are judged according to intention and that of the non-believers is directed toward worldly benefit alone.
- The ḥadīth shows that none will be destroyed by his wrongdoings except a rejecter of guidance and deliberately wicked person.
- Allah registers all deeds by means of angels. Scholars have differed over whether or not recording angels know the intentions of men. Perhaps they are informed by Allah what to write, as He has quoted them as saying: لَا عِلْمَ لَنَا إِلَّا مَا عَلَّمْتَنَا ***"No knowledge have we except what You have taught us."***[233]
- There is not mention in this ḥadīth of bad deeds done with good intentions or good deeds done with bad intentions. That subject has been dealt with in Ḥadīth No. 1.

---

232 An exception to this is noted in the Qur'ān (see 22:25). The mere intention from anywhere on earth to commit a sin in the Ḥaram of Makkah is sufficient to earn punishment from Allah, even if one fails to accomplish it.

233 Sūrah al-Baqarah, 2:32.

Hadīth No. 38

عن أبي هريرة قال: قال رسول الله (ﷺ):

« إنَّ الله تَعَالَى قَالَ: مَن عَادَى لِي وَلِيًّا فَقَد آذَنتُهُ بِالحَربِ. وَمَا تَقَرَّبَ إِلَيَّ عَبدِي بِشَيءٍ أَحَبُّ إِلَيَّ مِمَّا افتَرَضتُهُ عَلَيهِ، وَلاَ يَزَالُ عَبدِي يَتَقَرَّبُ إِلَيَّ بِالنَّوَافِلِ حَتَّى أُحِبَّهُ، فَإِذَا أَحبَبتُهُ كُنتُ سَمعَهُ الَّذِي يَسمَعُ بِهِ، وَبَصَرَهُ الَّذِي يُبصِرُ بِهِ، وَيَدَهُ الَّتِي يَبطِشُ بِهَا، وَرِجلَهُ الَّتِي يَمشِي بِهَا، وَلَئِن سَأَلَنِي لأُعطِيَنَّهُ، وَلَئِن استَعَاذَنِي لأُعِيذَنَّهُ»

On the authority of Abū Hurayrah, who said: The Messenger of Allah (ﷺ) said:

"Allah, the Exalted, has said,[234] 'Whoever is an enemy to My loyal friend – on him I declare war. My servant does not draw near to Me with anything more loved by Me than what [religious obligations] I have imposed on him. And My servant continues to draw near to Me with additional works until I love him; and when I love him, I am his hearing with which he hears, his sight with which he sees, his hand with which he strikes, and his foot with which he walks. If he asked [something] of Me, I would surely give it to him; and if he sought refuge with Me, I would surely grant it to him.'"

(Narrated by al-Bukhāri)

Here, the Prophet (ﷺ) reported that Allah has given severe warning to His enemies at every place and time who, since they are helpless against Him, seek to vent their hatred against his sincere and loyal servants. Then He (*subḥānahu wa ta'ālā*) described those servants, showing how they become close to Him and how He supports them in turn.

The "*wali*" (close and loyal friend or ally) of Allah has been defined in the Qur'ān:

الَّذِينَ آمَنُوا كَانُوا يَتَّقُونَ

"Those who believed and were conscious [of Allah]."[235]

It is a general term which includes all those who conscientiously adhere to the religion out of love for Allah and is not limited to scholars or those who have gained a reputation for piety among men.[236] Since any Muslim can be assumed to possess these qualities of faith and *taqwā*,[237] one should beware of animosity toward Muslims in general and of injury to their persons or their hearts.

The kind of animosity against which Allah has cautioned in this ḥadīth is that harbored toward a Muslim due to his loyalty to Allah and not difference over a right which might lead two believers to oppose one another in a court of law, or ordinary

234 See footnote no. 123.

235 Sūrah Yūnus, 10:63.

236 Unfortunately, the term "*wali*" has been misunderstood by many Muslims in recent times. Often translated as "saint," it has erroneously come to mean an exclusive status designated to a few, while the true extent of their righteousness can be known only to Allah. These are revered often to the point of shirk by the ignorant masses who make pilgrimages to their graves and even seek help or intercession from them. Worse, many of the so-called "saints" are now self-proclaimed or are completely fictitious characters around whom a cult is established.

237 See footnote no. 16.

rivalry and competition between them. This warning applies to any of the disbelievers or hypocrites who might resent a believer because of his religion and seek to harm him for that reason.

A declaration of war has been announced by Allah Himself upon anyone who hates or abuses a righteous believer, transgressing or plotting against his person, his property or his honor. And who can withstand the assault of Allah? He might extend the time of an oppressor but will never forget him. There can be no doubt that when Allah wages war against any creature, he will surely be destroyed.[238]

The loyal friends of Allah for whom He goes to war are those who have become close to Him through worship and obedience. They are of two kinds: those who draw near to Allah by fulfilling their obligations to Him and those who, after fulfilling their obligations, come yet closer through the voluntary good deeds which are pleasing to Him. Anyone who claims he can become a *wali* of Allah in some other way is obviously a liar.

The best and most beloved deeds to Allah are the religious obligations ordained by Him. Thus, they must always be given priority. It is these that earn the greatest reward, and they can never be replaced by voluntary worship of any kind.[239]

The foremost among religious obligations is abstention from everything which Allah has forbidden, for His anger over deliberate disobedience will not be appeased by good deeds of less importance. Moreover, a *nāfilah* or additional (voluntary) act of worship cannot even be defined as such until the *farīdhah* (obligation) has been fulfilled; otherwise, it will not be "additional," and in no way can it ever be a substitute. How unfortunate it is to observe the so-called "worshippers" who habitually fast and pray at night while neglecting the most basic obligations such as justice, truthfulness, kindness to parents, etc., which Allah (*subḥānahu wa ta'ālā*) has ordained in His Book. The servants who draw near to Allah are those who adhere to His ordinances of every kind and follow His directives in each matter to the best of their abilities, and to these Paradise has been guaranteed.

Then there are those who aspire to a higher position – yet closer to Allah. Perhaps they are acutely aware of sins they have committed or fearful that their worship is somehow deficient. It is they who embark upon a variety of supplementary deeds in addition to their obligations. The obvious advantage in doing so is to make up for imperfections in obligatory worship, as stated in several ḥadīths. In this way one's record of obedience is completed in the Hereafter, and what exceeds that is additional nearness to Allah. He (*subḥānahu wa ta'ālā*) has made clear the result in this worldly life as well: He will love His servant and guide him throughout his remaining days,

238 Let no one suppose because he, his family or his property apparently remain untouched that an enemy of Allah will escape His vengeance. A greater affliction could very well be a less obvious one, such as the sealing of his heart against the reception of truth and guidance with its evil consequence in the Hereafter.

239 This preference might be compared to that of a person who has made a specific request pertaining to an important matter. He is pleased upon its fulfillment and additionally pleased when something extra is offered beyond what he requested. However, if the initial request is ignored, he will not be pleased, even if something else is done for him instead.

protecting him from falling into sin and from the temptations of Shayṭān, insuring his entrance into Paradise with eternal nearness to Him in the life to come.

Allah's guidance of such a believer is reflected in all of his actions. He will continue in righteous deeds and avoid what is undesirable (*makrūh*) or of questionable status,[240] thereby elevating himself from the station of *īmān* to that of *iḥsān*.[241] Allah's will becomes the criterion by which he sees and hears, for what he does and which direction he takes. This is allegorically expressed as His "being" the servant's hearing, sight, hand and foot. Any explanation other than this can lead to deviation and disbelief. Such is the case of a number of misguided mystics who improperly interpret the ḥadīth to support the blasphemous concepts of *ḥulool* (the dwelling of Allah within creation) and *ittiḥād* (the union of creation and divinity). This is the very antithesis of *tawḥeed,* leading to the worship of creation instead of Allah alone, a dangerous form of *shirk* from which Allah and His Messenger (ﷺ) are disassociated entirely.

A further benefit derived from Allah's love is His protection from evil when refuge is sought in Him and immediate response to the believer's supplication.[242] Many of the Prophet's companions and their pious students were known to be readily answered by Allah. Yet, most of them did not supplicate for relief from personal afflictions but patiently endured, asking Allah for the good of whatever He decreed. Hence, their supplications for others and for the Muslim community at large had a visible effect.

---

240 In addition to what is prohibited (*ḥarām*). See Ḥadīth No. 11 and No. 12.

241 See Ḥadīth No. 2.

242 Response to a supplication will be in one of three forms: the granting of a request in this world, the preservation of it for the Hereafter, or the averting of a misfortune equal to the extent of one's supplication. (Related by Aḥmad with a *ḥasan* chain.) In part of a ḥadīth narrated by aṭ-Ṭabarāni and graded as *ḥasan*, the Prophet (ﷺ) is quoted as saying, *"Among my community are those who, if one of them asked Allah for Paradise, He would give it to him; and if he asked Allah for something from this world, He would not give him out of regard for him."*

Hadīth No. 39

عن ابن عباس أن رسول الله (ﷺ) قال:

«إِنَّ اللهَ تَجَاوَزَ لِي عَنْ أُمَّتِي الخَطَأَ، وَالنِّسيَانَ، وَمَا استُكرِهوا عَلَيهِ»

On the authority of Ibn 'Abbās that the Messenger of Allah (ﷺ) said:

"Allah has overlooked for me from my nation [what is done in] error and forgetfulness and what they are compelled to do."

(Ḥadīth *ḥasan* narrated by Ibn Mājah, al-Bayhaqi and others)

This ḥadīth is one of great benefit and contains reassurance for the believers concerning many matters in life. It shows the mercy of Allah in His alleviation of difficulties for the Muslim *ummah.* It is also the basis of an important *fiqh* ruling, which is that sin is incurred when there is willful intent. So when someone does what Allah has prohibited or fails to do what He has commanded without any willingness on his part, he is not subject to blame in this world or in the Hereafter.[243]

When Allah (*subḥānahu wa ta'ālā*) revealed the verse containing: ***"Whether you show what is within yourselves or conceal it – Allah will bring you to account for it,"***[244] the *ṣaḥābah* were distressed and said, "This is something we cannot bear." The Prophet (ﷺ) replied, "*Do you want to say as the people of the two scriptures before you said, 'We hear and disobey'? Rather, say,* ***'We hear and obey. Your forgiveness, our Lord, and to You is the destination.'***"[245] And when the people had recited it and their tongues became accustomed to it, Allah revealed: ***"Allah charges no soul except [with that within] its capacity. It will have what good it has gained and what evil it has earned. [Say], 'Our Lord, do not impose blame upon us if we have forgotten or erred...'"***[246]

Some elucidation is in order pertaining to the rulings of this ḥadīth:

1) What constitutes "error"

The word "*khata'*" (mistake or error), as used in this narration, means the opposite of intent and purpose, not the opposite of correctness. In other words, it is when a person, making a decision or acting in a certain manner, intends something but the result is other than what he expected. An example is the ruling of a judge who, while intending to uphold justice and exerting his utmost effort to arrive at the truth, might somehow be deceived by an appearance or by a skillful advocate. If he should happen to err through no fault of his own, he is even so rewarded for his righteous intent and effort. As reported in the two *Ṣaheeḥs* of al-Bukhāri and Muslim, the Prophet (ﷺ) said, "*When the judge rules after ijtihād*[247] *and is correct, he will have a double reward; and when he rules after ijtihād and errs, he will [still] have a reward.*"

---

243 For Qur'ānic evidences see 2:286, 16:106 and 33:5. One may, however, be held legally responsible for damages caused unwittingly.

244 Sūrah al-Baqarah, 2:284.

245 Sūrah al-Baqarah, 2:285.

246 Sūrah al-Baqarah, 2:286. The narration is by Muslim.

247 For definition, see footnote no. 59.

Al-Ḥasan al-Baṣri commented, "If Allah had not mentioned those two men [i.e., Prophets Dāwūd and Sulaymān], I would have thought that judges would be destroyed [for their errors], but Allah acclaimed one of them for his knowledge and excused the other because of his *ijtihad.*" And in fact, He praised them both.[248]

A second example is an accidental killing, which usually results from an error in judgement. During *jihād,* a man might kill one whom he assumes to be an enemy and later come to know that he was a believer. Or, in a fit of anger, someone might strike a person without the intention to kill, yet causing his death either directly or indirectly.[249] Or a death might occur as the result of an error made by someone while no harm was intended to anyone at all. Although the killer is absolved from the sin of intent and is therefore not subject to execution, he remains responsible for legal reparation as described in the Qur'ān (4:92) and can surely be held accountable for any lesser harm intended and for the careless negligence leading to a death. The same applies to unintentional destruction of property and other forms of harm or injury, which must be compensated in the interest of justice unless forgiven by the victim.

2) The meaning of "forgetfulness"

The Arabic word "*nisyān*" refers to a temporary state of having completely forgotten something and not, as some assume, to forgetfulness as a trait or tendency. Hence, failure to remember in spite of the intention to do so is overlooked by Allah, while carelessness in this regard remains blameworthy. For example, due to unusual circumstances one might forget a prayer until its period has expired, although he is normally most conscientious about praying on time. Such a one incurs no sin, although he is not excused from performing the missed prayer and must do so as soon as he remembers.[250] In contrast, one who delays and procrastinates without necessity at the beginning of the period until he finally forgets towards its end is at least partially guilty since he abandoned the care required to insure the fulfillment of his obligation.[251]

A general rule for matters of error and forgetfulness is that if it occurs regarding a prescribed duty, it must be done as soon as there is realization that it was not performed. If it occurs regarding a prohibition wherein no damage is caused, it is excused. But if it results in loss, harm or injury to another, compensation is required unless the injured party forgoes his right. Hence, the conclusion is obvious: that the negation of sin does not necessarily mean the negation of responsibility for the consequence.

3) The types and extent of "compulsion"

Rulings pertaining to compulsion differ according to its extent and the nature of the

---

248 Refer to Sūrah al-Anbiyā', 21:78-79.

249 As did Mūsā in the time before his prophethood. See Sūrah al-Qaṣaṣ, 28:15.

250 Al-Imām Muslim narrated: The Prophet (ﷺ) said, "*Whoever has forgotten a prayer or slept through its time should pray it when he remembers it, and there is no expiation for it except that.*" Al-Bukhāri reported similar words.

251 The same applies to sleep. If one remains oblivious despite his efforts to insure awakening in time for prayer, no sin is committed as long as he performs the missed prayer as soon as he is aware of it. However, failure to request that someone awaken him or to set an alarm shows a measure of carelessness.

deed. For compulsion might be total, such as the case of one who is tied up or drugged and then carried bodily to a place he had sworn he would never enter. The consensus here is that he has not incurred any sin and is not responsible for the expiation of his oath. But more often it is of the type in which a person has the ability to resist, although his choice may be limited by a threat to himself or others for whom he cares. Such cases are varied and can only be judged in the light of each circumstance.[252] Perhaps human judgement could be deemed fair when it gives the benefit of a doubt, but Allah alone knows the absolute truth of every matter.

Refusal to comply in what is sinful despite a severe threat is rewarded, but it is not obligatory. One exception is murder, for most scholars have ruled that when a person's life is threatened unless he in turn kills another, it does not become permissible for him to do so to save himself. All lesser forms of disobedience committed unwillingly under the threat of death or disastrous consequences are not considered to be accountable sins.

There is a consensus concerning speech – that anyone compelled to make a statement against his will shall not be held responsible as long as he does not act upon it. This is clear from Allah's revelation regarding the companion who uttered words of disbelief under extreme duress and then despaired of forgiveness.[253] Since the revealed alleviation pertained to *kufr* (disbelief), the greatest of sins, lesser ones cannot be excluded.

From here it is concluded as well that promises, agreements or transactions contracted under compulsion are invalid. However, when a person is compelled by a court of law to do what is right and just, it is valid and must be upheld. And Allah knows best.

---

252 For example, scholars have ruled that a woman overpowered and forced to endure a sexual assault commits no sin. However, one who submits while able to resist is judged according to the nature of the threat against her.

253 See Sūrah an-Naḥl, 16:106.

Ḥadīth No. 40

عن ابن عمر قال:

أَخَذَ رَسُولُ اللهِ (ﷺ) بِمَنْكِبِي فَقَالَ: «كُنْ فِي الدُّنْيَا كَأَنَّكَ غَرِيبٌ أَوْ عَابِرُ سَبِيلٍ»

وكان ابن عمر يقول: «إِذَا أَمْسَيْتَ فَلاَ تَنْتَظِرِ الصَّبَاحَ، وَإِذَا أَصْبَحْتَ فَلاَ تَنْتَظِرِ المَسَاءَ، وَخُذْ مِنْ صِحَّتِكَ لِمَرَضِكَ وَمِنْ حَيَاتِكَ لِمَوْتِكَ»

On the authority of Ibn ʿUmar, who said:

The Messenger of Allah (ﷺ) took me by the shoulder and said, "Be in the world as though you were a stranger or a wayfarer."

And Ibn ʿUmar used to say, "When you have reached the evening, do not await the morning; and when you have reached morning, do not await the evening. Take from your health for your illness and from your life for your death."

(Narrated by al-Bukhāri)

The Prophet's instruction to ʿAbdullāh, the son of ʿUmar bin al-Khaṭṭāb, is counted among the comprehensive ḥadīths which cover many aspects of life. It is supported by a number of other narrations similar in meaning[254] that warn against becoming overly attached to this world, which is not a real home but only a temporary station. In fact, it is actually a barrier between a man and his permanent residence, keeping him away from it until the time willed by Allah. In taking Ibn ʿUmar by the shoulder, the Prophet (ﷺ) showed affection for him but was also drawing his attention to the importance of the knowledge he was about to impart, insuring that his student would always remember the instruction and pass it on to others.

The Messenger of Allah (ﷺ) encouraged Ibn ʿUmar and all believers to adopt a traveler's state of mind – that of one who does not carry more than what he requires during his journey so as not to be burdened and perhaps prevented from reaching his destination. His main concern is the final destination – what he will find there and how he will secure for himself an environment of comfort and satisfaction. Allah (subḥānahu wa taʿālā) has said:

وَلْتَنظُرْ نَفْسٌ مَا قَدَّمَتْ لِغَدٍ

"And let every soul look to what it has put forth for tomorrow..."[255]

So the intelligent believer is not deluded by the worldly life, nor does he give it undue importance or feel secure therein. Rather, he recognizes that it is a time of preparation and of sowing the seeds of good to be reaped in the final abode. The temporary nature of this life was emphasized by the Prophet (ﷺ) when he said, "*What does the world mean to me? It is only like the shade of a tree in which a rider naps at noon; then he moves on and leaves it behind.*"[256]

Among those who lived this concept was the companion Abū Dharr al-Ghifāri. A man entered his house and after looking about said, "Where are your furnishings?" He

---

254 Such as Ḥadīth No. 31 of this collection.
255 Sūrah al-Ḥashr, 59:18.
256 Related by Aḥmad and at-Tirmidhī, who graded it as ḥasan-ṣaḥeeḥ.

replied, "I have another house to which I direct [concern]." The visitor said, "But you must have furnishings [or provisions] as long as you remain here." He replied, "The Owner of this house has not invited me to remain in it." Another righteous man was told, "Your house looks as if it belonged to someone about to leave. Will you be leaving?" He replied, "Rather, I will be evicted."

Being as a stranger implies a state of caution and unease, for he is unfamiliar with the customs of the local people and uncertain of their hospitality. When passing through a town and meeting some of its inhabitants, a stranger will not worry about being seen in a less than perfect state or attempt to compete with people in their gatherings or dispute and fight with them since his stay is brief and his concerns are other than those of the people around him. Some scholars have suggested that the ḥadīth discourages excessive socializing in the world, as a stranger or traveler feels alone among those he does not know, and perhaps even humble or fearful. But Allah knows best.

Thus, the believer will take from this world – out of dwellings, possessions and companions – whatever will ease his passage to the next. He will see his life as a mere crossing but also as an opportunity to obtain for himself the best of the eternal home for which he longs, much as the stranger or traveler longs for his home and family after a long absence. When reflecting, he will ask himself: "How can I rejoice in the world while its days deplete my remaining months, its months deplete my remaining years, and its years deplete my life? How can I rejoice in that which steers my life to its term and drives me on towards death, leaving me nothing of its fleeting pleasures?" The servant's stay is one of numbered days, each passing day reducing it and hastening its end. As the believing man stated to the subjects of Pharaoh:

يَاقَومِ إِنَّمَا هَٰذِهِ الحَيَاةُ الدُّنيَا مَتَاعٌ وَإِنَّ الآخِرَةَ هِيَ دَارُ القَرَارِ

"O my people, this worldly life is but temporary enjoyment, and indeed, the Hereafter – that is the home of permanent settlement."[257]

The advice given by Ibn 'Umar is based upon the ḥadīth which he related. From his understanding of the transitory nature of life on earth, he concluded that a Muslim should be constantly prepared for death, expecting it could come at any moment and never assuming that he has plenty of time to eventually fulfill his obligations to Allah and his fellow men or to repent from sin. When one reduces his hope of living even until the following morning or evening, it will reduce his aspiration for worldly acquisitions. He will seek instead to use whatever precious time he has left for amending his affairs and earning the acceptance of Allah, for if he uses his remaining time badly, he will be blamed for that and for what preceded; but if he uses it well, he will be rewarded for it and forgiven for what preceded.

An effective method for perfecting one's work is to imagine that each deed could be the last while remembering that everyone will be resurrected in accordance with the state in which he died.[258] Thus, the servant of Allah will hasten to accomplish one more

---

257 Sūrah Ghāfir, 40:39.

258 This was reported in a ḥadīth narrated by Muslim.

good deed after another, never postponing what is possible to do immediately and striving to make it the best that he is able.

The other recommendation by Ibn `Umar is that a person make the most of every opportunity, not for worldly gain, but to perform his religious obligations and put forth as much good as possible for benefit in the Hereafter. Perhaps he was referring to another ḥadīth in which the Prophet (ﷺ) said, "*Avail yourself of five things before five: your life before your death, your health before your illness, your free time before your busy time, your youth before your old age, and your wealth before your poverty.*"[259] There is great advantage in increasing good deeds during times of ability because one will continue to earn reward for them in times of disability. Allah commands the recording angels, "*Register for My servant during every day and night whatever good he used to do for as long as he is confined in My restriction.*"[260] Such periods of ability are favors from Allah that should not be wasted. As His Messenger (ﷺ) said, "*There are two blessings of which many people are deprived: health and free time.*"[261]

Life itself is an opportunity. For once a person dies, his work is ended, his hope is lost, and upon resurrection he will only regret what he had once neglected. Al-Imām al-Ghazāli said, "The body is as a fishnet, used to collect good, but it will be taken away at death." Everyone should know that he will face a long period under the ground when he will be unable to do a single thing, so let him make good use of his days on earth. `Ali bin Abī Ṭālib remarked, "Today is the time for deeds with no account. Then there will be a time of account and no deeds."

When concentrating on the final home, however, the Muslim cannot abandon the world and its necessities any more than the traveler can neglect the upkeep of his means of transport. What is blameworthy is only an excessive attachment and devotion to the world and forgetting that one will soon move on to the greater eternal life, the quality of which depends directly upon his careful preparations in this temporary encampment. Hard work and effort are required to give self-sufficiency, obtain benefit and assist others, and with the correct intention become a part of the good work rewarded by Allah in the permanent abode as well as in the present one.

259 Narrated by al-Ḥākim – ṣaḥeeḥ.
260 Narrated by al-Ḥākim – ṣaḥeeḥ.
261 Narrated by al-Bukhāri.

Hadīth No. 41

عن أبي محمد عبد الله بن عمرو بن العاص قال: قال رسول الله (ﷺ):

« لاَ يُؤمِنُ أَحَدُكُم حَتَّى يَكُونَ هَوَاهُ تَبَعًا لِمَا جِئتُ بِهِ»

On the authority of Abū Muḥammad, `Abdullāh the son of 'Amr bin al-'Aas, who said: The Messenger of Allah (ﷺ) said:

"None of you [truly] believes until his inclination is in accordance with what I have brought."

(A *ḥasan-ṣaḥeeḥ* ḥadīth transmitted from *Kitāb al-Ḥujjah* with a *ṣaḥeeḥ* chain)[262]

The few words of this ḥadīth encompass Islam in its entirety and define true faith. Al-Imām an-Nawawi said, "It means that a person must measure his deeds against the Qur'ān and *sunnah,* oppose his own inclinations, and follow what the Prophet (ﷺ) conveyed. And it is similar to the saying of Allah, the Exalted:

وَمَا كَانَ لِمُؤمِنٍ وَلاَ مُؤمِنَةٍ إِذَا قَضَى اللهُ وَرَسُولُهُ أَمرًا أَن يَكُونَ لَهُمُ الخِيَرَةُ مِن أَمرِهِم

"It is not for a believing man or a believing woman, when Allah and His Messenger have decided a matter, that they have the choice about their affair."[263]

A Muslim cannot have complete faith until he likes all that Allah and His Messenger like and dislikes all that they dislike, which means that the sincere believer will be pleased to obey Allah and careful about doing it correctly and precisely. It follows that anyone who claims to love Allah, yet does not respect His limits and obey His commands as taught by His Messenger (ﷺ), is not only untruthful but exposes the weakness of his faith. Just as true faith requires living and practicing the religion according to the Prophet's sunnah, it also requires submitting willingly to the laws of the *Sharī`ah* and accepting it as the criterion by which to judge all matters.[264] Allah (*subḥānahu wa ta`ālā*) said:

مَن يُطِعِ الرَسُولَ فَقَد أَطَاعَ الله

"Whoever obeys the Messenger has obeyed Allah."[265]

The word "*hawā*" used in this ḥadīth is related to a verb meaning "fall" and is defined as the desire of the self for something or its inclination toward what it likes or what suits it. Its general implication is a negative one: the seeking of immediate gratification without regard for consequences. Thus, it is mentioned in the Qur'ān as something to be resisted and opposed,[266] and which may, when unchecked, even

---

262 *Kitāb al-Ḥujjah* is a book outlining the fundamentals of the religion according to the principles of Ahl as-Sunnah written by Abul-Faṭḥ, Naṣr bin Ibrāheem al-Maqdisi. In his commentary Imām Ibn Rajab expressed doubts about the authenticity of this ḥadīth due to weakness in the chain of narrators. Shaykh al-Albāni has also noted the same weakness. The meaning is correct, however, supported by other ḥadīths and several Qur'ānic verses. (Refer to Ḥadīths No. 5 and No. 28 of this collection.)

263 Sūrah al-Aḥzāb, 33:36.

264 Refer to Sūrah an-Nisaa', 4:65.

265 Sūrah an-Nisaa', 4:80.

266 For example, see 4:135, 6:119, 18:28, 28:50, 38:26, 45:18 and 79:40.

become a rival to Allah – obeyed instead of Him.[267] Every kind of disobedience and blameworthy innovation results from giving preference to inclinations that differ from what the Messenger (ﷺ) has conveyed from Allah. Being somewhat less than complete believers, many people will need to make a conscious effort to oppose such desires and inclinations that, encouraged by Shayṭān, tempt one away from the straight path and can lead him into various degrees of deviation or disobedience.

The usage of the word here, however, points to the fact that inclinations can indeed be conditioned and changed. It also shows that "*hawā*" can mean love in a positive sense as well, such as love for the truth. Hence, a person who is certain in faith will realize that what was conveyed by the Prophet (ﷺ) is beneficial to him in this world and the next, and his conviction will make that way of life desirable to him to the exclusion of all others.

267 See 25:43 and 45:23. This kind of *shirk* is probably the most common in every age.

Ḥadīth No. 42

عن أنس قال: سمعت رسول الله (ﷺ) يقول:

« قَالَ اللهُ تَعَالَى: يَا ابْنَ آدَمَ، إِنَّكَ مَا دَعَوْتَنِي وَرَجَوْتَنِي غَفَرْتُ لَكَ عَلَى مَا كَانَ مِنْكَ وَلاَ أُبَالِي. يَا ابْنَ آدَمَ، لَوْ بَلَغَتْ ذُنُوبُكَ عَنَانَ السَّمَاءِ ثُمَّ اسْتَغْفَرْتَنِي، غَفَرْتُ لَكَ. يَا ابْنَ آدَمَ، إِنَّكَ لَوْ أَتَيْتَنِي بِقُرَابِ الأَرْضِ خَطَايَا ثُمَّ لَقِيتَنِي لاَ تُشْرِكُ بِي شَيْئًا، لَأَتَيْتُكَ بِقُرَابِهَا مَغْفِرَةً. »

On the authority of Anas, who said: I heard the Messenger of Allah (ﷺ) say:

"Allah, the Exalted, has said, 'O son of Ādam, as long as you supplicate Me and implore Me, I will forgive for you whatever issued from you, and I will not mind. O son of Ādam, even if your sins reached the clouds of the sky and then you sought My forgiveness, I would forgive you. O son of Ādam, even if you come to Me with nearly the earth's capacity of sins and then meet Me without associating anything with Me, I will come to you with nearly its capacity of forgiveness.'" [268]

(Narrated by at-Tirmidhi, who said it was a ḥasan-ṣaḥeeḥ ḥadīth)

This *ḥadīth qudsi*[269] has been described as the most encouraging and reassuring narration in the sunnah, for it contains good tidings for every believer who fears Allah and worships none but Him. Three causes are cited which lead to Allah's forgiveness through repentance and *tawḥeed*. Each will be mentioned in turn:

1) Allah (*subḥānahu wa ta'ālā*) has directed His servants to *du`aa'* (supplication) accompanied by *rajaa'*, which encompasses the meanings of both fear and hope. One who has sinned should thus supplicate Allah fearful of punishment for what he committed, knowing that it is deserved by him, apologizing, and humbly begging for his Lord's mercy and pardon. At the same time he entertains the hope that Allah, the all-Merciful, will regard his deep regret and generously overlook his many errors and sins. Some commentators have emphasized this aspect over fear, observing that *rajaa'* also means expectation, i.e., of Allah's response.

وَقَالَ رَبُّكُمُ ادْعُونِي أَسْتَجِبْ لَكُمْ

"And your Lord said, 'Call upon Me; I will answer you.'"[270]

The combination of fear and hope leads one to supplicate sincerely, intently and often, which is pleasing to Allah and evidence of belief in His awareness and mercy. Hence, Allah forgives the servant's sins, even those of which he may have been unaware.

But everyone should know that Allah (*subḥānahu wa ta'ālā*) does not accept a supplication for something sinful or for cutting off relations between relatives or that of one who willfully obtains and consumes what is prohibited.[271] Supplications by the tongue alone while the heart is absent are weak and therefore unlikely to bring

---

268 i.e., with forgiveness equal to the amount of sins committed. Forgiveness (*maghfirah*) is defined as "the concealment of a sin by Allah and protection from its evil effects in the Hereafter."
269 See footnote no. 123 to Ḥadīth No. 24.
270 Sūrah Ghāfir, 40:60.
271 Refer to Ḥadīth No. 10.

response, as are those of persons persistent in sin and unwilling to desist. On the other hand, the generally righteous person, drawing near to Allah through earnest supplication, can expect to be answered sooner or later, as Allah wills,[272] for He has said:

وَادعُوهُ خَوفًا وَطَمَعًا إِنَّ رَحمَتَ اللهِ قَرِيبٌ مِنَ المُحسِنِينَ

"*And invoke Him in fear and aspiration. Indeed, the mercy of Allah is near to the doers of good.*"[273]

2) The second cause of earning Allah's forgiveness is seeking it and asking for it (*istighfār*). Again, this is not an act of the tongue alone but must be accompanied by true repentance.[274] The merits of seeking forgiveness from Allah are mentioned in numerous Qur'ānic verses and other ḥadīths, such as that related by al-Bukhāri in which the Prophet (ﷺ) taught his companions the best supplication for forgiveness.[275]

3) The third condition is that the servant not associate anyone or anything with Allah in any aspect of His divinity, knowing that none is worthy of worship except Him. For Allah has said in the Qur'ān:

إِنَّ اللهَ لاَ يَغفِرُ أَن يُشرَكَ بِهِ وَيَغفِرُ مَا دُونَ ذٰلِكَ لِمَن يَشَاءُ

"*Indeed, Allah does not forgive that anything be associated with Him, but He forgives what is less than that for whom He wills.*"[276]

Thus, when *tawḥeed* is lost, forgiveness is lost as well; and when it is affirmed by the Muslim, it will earn him the Prophet's intercession, Allah's forgiveness, and will save him from the Hellfire. This can mean either of two things: that he is forgiven and thus prevented from entering it at all, or, that after entering due to the gravity of his sins and enduring a portion of his deserved punishment, Allah will forgive him and he will be removed therefrom and placed in Paradise, while the disbelievers, hypocrites and those who associated others in worship with Allah will remain in Hell eternally. It is confirmed in the narration by al-Bukhāri, wherein the Prophet (ﷺ) disclosed, that finally "*Allah will command that anyone who said 'Lā illāh ill-Allāh' and whose heart contained good the weight of a barley or wheat grain be removed from the Fire.*" Thus, the scholars have declared that *tawḥeed* is the major cause of salvation, for its people will all eventually enter Paradise.[277] And if such is the case for the sinful of this *ummah,* what can the righteous expect, those who uphold *tawḥeed,* worship and obey Allah throughout their lives, and avoid the major sins? Surely they can look forward to forgiveness of their major sins, protection from Hellfire altogether, and immediate entrance into Paradise. What greater success and what greater favor?

---

272 See footnote no. 244.

273 Sūrah al-A`rāf, 7:56.

274 Refer to commentary on Ḥadīth No. 18 and No. 24 for requirements of repentance.

275 "*O Allah, You are my Lord – there is no god but You. You created me and I am Your servant; and I upheld Your covenant and [my] promise to You as much as I am able. I seek refuge in You from the evil I have done. I acknowledge to You Your favor upon me, and I acknowledge my sin, so forgive me. For indeed, there is none who can forgive sins except You.*"

276 Sūrah an-Nisaa', 4:48 and 4:116.

277 No one having belief in the realities of Hellfire could make light of even a temporary stay, as did the Jews described in Sūrah al-Baqarah, 2:80.

It must be noted that each of the three aforementioned causes of forgiveness is a requirement. The first two are ineffectual without the third, for although Allah (*subḥānahu wa ta'ālā*) may forgive what He pleases for whom He wills of those who affirm His right to be worshipped exclusively, He has stated that He will not forgive *shirk* (association), the greatest sin. And the third condition, being the first pillar of Islam, is inclusive of every aspect of life.[278] No person should be deluded into thinking that mere utterance of the *kalimah*, "*Lā illāh ill-Allāh*" is sufficient, for that phrase must reflect sincere belief proven by effort.[279] Otherwise it becomes a statement of hypocrisy, and Allah is concerned with what is in the heart, and He is most knowing of His servants.

* * * * *

This concludes the collection of comprehensive Prophetic narrations compiled by al-Imām Yaḥyā bin Sharaf an-Nawawi, may Allah have mercy upon him. And to Allah is due all praise and gratitude.

---

278 The disbelievers of Quraysh understood this fact well when they refused even to pronounce the shahādah.

279 See commentary to Ḥadīth No. 3.

www.ingramcontent.com/pod-product-compliance
Lightning Source LLC
LaVergne TN
LVHW020423080526
838202LV00055B/5015